Toward a Truly Free Market

Culture of Enterprise series

Toward a Truly Free Market

A Distributist Perspective on the Role of Government, Taxes, Health Care, Deficits, and More

John C. Médaille

Wilmington, Delaware

Copyright © 2010 by John C. Médaille
Paperback edition, 2011
Paperback ISBN: 9781610170277

The Culture of Enterprise series is supported by a grant from the John Templeton Foundation. The Intercollegiate Studies Institute gratefully acknowledges this support.

Médaille, John C.

    Toward a truly free market : a distributist perspective on the role of government, taxes, health care, deficits, and more / John C. Médaille.
    p. cm.
    ISBN 1-935191-81-0

       1. Distributive justice. 2. Economics—Social aspects. 3. Economic policy—Social aspects. 4. Capitalism—Social aspects. 5. Free enterprise—Social aspects. I. Title.

HB523.M43 2010
330.1—dc22   2010010598

Published in the United States by:

ISI Books
Intercollegiate Studies Institute
3901 Centerville Road
Wilmington, Delaware 19807-1938
www.isibooks.org

Manufactured in the United States of America

Contents

1

What's in a Name?

The most important thing, the first thing, in understanding anything is to get the name right. If you and I were to have a conversation on any subject, say horses, and you were to refer to them as "dogs" and I were to call them "cats," there is a good chance that some misunderstandings might arise—misunderstandings that could never be resolved until we decided to agree on a name for the thing we were talking about. This book is an attempt to make clear certain matters concerning the material relations between men, and to correct what I see as the greatest errors in the field that deals with these matters, the field known as *economics*. But before I could correct anyone else's errors, I had to correct my own. This book started with an essay that was published in the *Distributist Review*, entitled "The Economics of Distributism." But as I searched the text for errors, both theoretical and grammatical, I suddenly realized that I had missed the biggest error of all—the very title. This book, which grows out of that essay, has a slightly different title, but in that slight difference is a world of difference. I let the title of the essay stand, because *economics* has become the term under which most men recognize the topic, and because I did not have space to explain the difference within the bounds of the essay. But in a book I may at least make the topic clear, even if I can do nothing else. And my topic is *political economy*, which is to say, the only kind of economy that actually exists.

Economics vs. Political Economy

Economics is, of course, a discipline which has an enormous amount of power and prestige. But one thing it does not have is a history, or at least not much of a history; the term *economics* is of comparatively recent origin. None of the great political economists of the nineteenth century were familiar with the term *economics*. For Adam Smith, David Ricardo, Karl Marx, Jean-Baptiste Say, Nassau Senior, John Stuart Mill, et al., their science was *political economy*. In fact, the twenty-volume *Oxford English Dictionary*—begun in 1878, completed in 1928, and meant to be the final resource on all English words—does not even have an entry for *economics*, neither in the main portion nor in the supplement. Given the recent provenance of the word, it is important to understand how and why it got here. The term, in its modern sense, may have first been suggested by the British prime minister Benjamin Disraeli in 1844 as a way of separating the political economy from the pesky topic of morals. It did not gain any currency until 1890 with the publication of A. E. Marshall's *Principles of Economics,* which begins, "Political Economy, or Economics, is a study of man's actions in the ordinary business of life. . . ."[1] Note that Marshall uses the old term before the new one and makes them out to be synonyms.

But if they were synonyms, there would be no reason for the change. The difference between the terms is that the political economists saw their science as a humane science firmly embedded in human institutions. The new *economists*, on the other hand, saw their discipline not as a humane science, but as something in the order of the physical sciences, which operate independently of human intentions. They wished to "free" the discipline from all social contexts. Of course, the first casualty of this "freedom" was freedom itself, since the markets were now moved in the same way as were the stars: by inexorable forces whose course no man could alter. It is ironic to hear otherwise intelligent men speak of the "free" market while denying its very freedom.

The problem with the new economists was not so much that they were wrong, but that they were very nearly right. There are certain tendencies in human beings that allow us to make lawlike statements. People do tend to buy more of a product when it is cheaper, and they tend to make more of that product when it is dearer; between these two tendencies, we really can posit supply and demand curves, and we can, at least in the abstract, discover the equilibrium point between these tendencies. And while the result of our calculations will not be a law in the sense that gravity is a law, in that it cannot be violated, it will be lawlike: that is, useful enough for us to give useful descriptions of a particular economy. All of this is true. But the real difficulties in human thought come not so much as an argument between truth and error (pure error is too easy to spot), but between greater truths and lesser truths. Correct thought is a matter of arranging truths in their proper hierarchies, of not allowing a lesser truth to displace a greater, or of not reducing all truths to one truth. This last error is the besetting sin of economists because, to make economics work as physics works, guided by physical measurement and ruled by pure mathematics, they have to reduce man to a physical object in a world of physical objects. They have to reduce man's labor to a mere commodity, purchased at the lowest value like any commodity; they have to reduce man to an economic calculator, the mythical *homo œconomicus*. Mostly, they have to divorce the economic question, as Disraeli desired, from any question of ethics. But one cannot found a science on a myth. Nor can one reduce man to something he clearly is not, or at least is not completely. Man occupies a moral universe as well as a physical one, and to ignore the place he occupies is to lose the man and hence lose the science. Man, in his relations with other men, is guided by whatever notions of justice he has. Even the man who claims to divorce the questions of morals from the economy will always be attempting to give a moral justification for his actions; the plutocrat who exploits his workers will rationalize it by claiming that in the end the exploitation adds to the commonweal, or that he is simply acting under the forces of "economic" nature. But if there is no question of justice, why bother to justify it?

Without understanding the nature of man, we cannot hope to understand the nature of his economic relations. The new "scientists" hoped to trade good justice for better science, but it was a bad bargain; in losing one they lost both. In losing the ability to properly describe their subject (the human person) they lost the ability to properly describe anything about him, and most especially his economic systems. They ended up not with a science, which could serve as an arbiter of questions disputed under the terms of the science, but with a series of warring ideologies among which there can be no arbitration, indeed no communication, because they have no common terms and no common understandings.

I want to be very clear here that I am not denying economic science. Indeed, I am affirming it. I am, however, denying that it is a physical science; I deny that it can draw its proper methodology from physics, astronomy, chemistry, or any other physical science. I affirm that it must be a humane science and use the methods of those sciences. In a later chapter, we will delve more deeply into the implications of this. For the moment, we can say that the humane sciences all rest in some vision of human justice, because justice is the virtue that regulates proper relations between man and man, between a man and his society. If we lose justice, and most particularly *distributive* justice, we lose any hope of science; indeed, we lose any hope for society. Here then, is the over-riding theme of this book: Economics, or more properly, political economy, cannot be a proper science unless it is a humane science; to be a humane science it must embody some notion of justice, and particularly of distributive justice. Indeed, as a practical matter as well as a theoretical one, there can be no balance between supply and demand without distributive justice; the moral question and the economic question are, in reality, one question. Economic equilibrium cannot be divorced from economic equity, and the attempt to do so will lose both equity and equilibrium; the economy will be unable to balance itself, and so will either fall to ruin, or to ruinous government attempts to redress the balance.

The Failure of the Economists

Our nation—and the world—is currently in the midst of a grave economic crisis. One salient fact about this crisis is that 90 percent of all economists failed to note the coming of this disaster. Further, those few who did give a warning were marginalized and ridiculed as "Dr. Dooms." While it is certainly true that some of those who sounded the alarm are perpetual naysayers, always crying wolf even in the best of times, it is not true of all of them. Further, it does not tell us why the bulk of the profession failed to note the coming of this train wreck. Nor should we be surprised by this failure, since 90 percent missed the coming of the last disaster, and the one before that, etc. Indeed, the record of the economists in predicting economic failures is nearly perfect: they have missed all of them.

With that disheartening statistic in mind, it would seem that we have some warrant for suspecting that the science of economics is, at this stage, incomplete, and hence incapable of giving a complete description of any economy. And if it cannot describe an economy, it cannot predict its course. Most importantly, however, such an incomplete science will not be able to make any rational policy prescriptions, and any prescriptions it does make are only likely to make the problems worse, to deepen and lengthen the recession. Therefore, our first task is one of understanding. We must examine the historical and theoretical roots of the science and correct what errors we find. Only then can we deal rationally with the problems at hand.

The Failure of the Distributists

Although this book is a critique of modern economics, it must start with a critique of modern distributists. I say "modern" distributists because distributism itself is nothing more than the rediscovery of an older view of economics. Until the sixteenth century, there was no real dispute that economics was a colony of ethics, rooted in the political order and dependent on distributive justice. No philosopher or theologian worthy of his stipend, beginning with Aristotle, was without his economic commentary. He felt it merely part of his natural function to comment on the real affairs of real men, and the economic and political orders were simply part of that commentary. Very nearly the full weight of human opinion, taken as a whole, comes down on the side of the distributists. While distributism adds to modern economics precisely what it lacks to become to a real science—the science of political economy—distributists themselves have often been reluctant to put their case in economic terms. The distributists have often argued from moral terms; they have placed their arguments in the necessary connection between free property and free men; they have argued on agrarian terms, on the natural rhythms of life and social order often disrupted by modern capitalism; they have argued from Roman Catholic teaching and the social encyclicals. But on the whole, they have been unwilling, or (I'm afraid) unable, to enter the economic debate on purely economic terms.

This is not a new problem. G. K. Chesterton and Hilaire Belloc, though they had an intuitive feel for political economy, lacked both the training and the interest to formulate a purely economic theory. Belloc's *The Servile State* was a shrewd critique of the economic order of his day, and it has proved prophetic about the decay of that order into a quasi-socialist order, dependent on big government, which is itself dependent on big capital. But even after *The Servile State*, neither *The Restoration of Property* nor *Economics for Helen* was of sufficient depth, economically, to establish distributism as a separate and distinct economic theory. Likewise, Chesterton's *What's Wrong with the World* and other writings showed great economic insight but little economic theorizing. This is unfortunate because the great opponents of the distributists in Chesterton's time, the Fabian socialists, insisted on first-class economic research. Although both Chesterton and Belloc were popular figures, and distributism a popular movement, the Fabians were able to carry the day because they could focus the debate on purely economic grounds, grounds the distributists were reluctant to enter.

This is not to deny that some great economists have been guided by the same principles as distributism. John Ryan, Heinrich Pesch, E. F. Schumacher, R. H. Tawney, and many others have made great contributions to our understanding of the political economy. Nor is this to deny that distributist practice has had tremendous successes: the long-standing success of the Mondragón Cooperative Corporation, with its fifty-year history and eighty thousand worker-owners; the remarkable distributive economy of Emilia-Romagna, where 40 percent of the GDP is from cooperative firms, and where the standard of living is one of the highest in Europe; the "land to the tiller" program of Taiwan, which lifted that nation from grinding poverty to economic power-house in only one generation; the success of so many Employee Stock Ownership Plans (ESOPs); and the success of micro-lending programs across the world. Indeed, distributist principles go from triumph to triumph, while capitalist societies go from government bailout to government bailout.

Despite these successes in both theory and practice, however, it is too often the case that in any discussion of economics the distributist is likely to be the least well-versed in the science; he is, too often, the one least able to place his argument in economic terms, and too ready to retreat to moral arguments. This has unfortunate consequences for distributism as a movement. First, we often fail to convince others of the *economic* soundness of our case. Second, those distributists who have an interest in economics find insufficient sustenance in distributism, and often drift off to Austrianism, Keynesianism, or socialism, theories which are nearly the opposite of distributism. Finally, we cannot recognize the similarities between our own positions and allied positions like mutualism and Georgism. In failing to recognize these similarities, we fail to recognize our natural allies. We even fail to recognize, too often, that which is valid and useful in neoclassical and Keynesian theories. All of this gives distributism a parochial cast. We end up marginalizing our own theory, simply because we often have a marginal understanding of the theory.

If the distributist would only enter the economic lists, he would find weapons and armor enough to stand against any opponent. Our theory is competitive at the intellectual level and thoroughly demonstrated at the practical level; we fill the gaps in the *science* of political economy that neoclassical economics, and all its variants, cannot. We do not need to stand on the margins, but in the mainstream. In this particular historical moment, when capitalism itself seems to be in crisis, we need to make our voices heard, and heard in a language the world can understand. This book is not the great tome that distributist political economy deserves (that is a task above my abilities and one that I leave to the next Pesch, Tawney, or Schumacher); it is intended to give the nonspecialist reader the intellectual arms and armor necessary to enter the debate on more equal terms.

2

If It Ain't Broke . . .

Does Capitalism Work?

Distributism calls for a reform of economic systems in general, and capitalism in particular. And yet, what is the point of calling for reform in a system that works, which is fully functional? Here, common wisdom must guide us, namely, "If it ain't broke, don't fix it!" At this point, many people would interrupt to say, "Just look around you, dummy. Of course it works! We are the richest and most powerful nation in the world, thanks to capitalism and the free market. Further, our system is so successful that it has been adopted by every prosperous nation in the world—even Communist China!" Well, it would be hard to dispute that America is a powerful country; what is not so clear is that it is a capitalist country, or has been one, for some time now.

In asking the question of whether or not capitalism is broke, I do not mean that there are certain imperfections in it, or that from time to time it experiences difficulties. It would be unreasonable, indeed churlish, to demand from any great system a standard of perfection that human beings and human systems simply do not have. And since we

11

must allow for imperfections, we must ask, "How do we judge whether capitalism—or any other system—is working?" Let me suggest that the most unassailable standard of judgment for any system is the standard that adherents of the system establish for themselves. We could criticize capitalists on any number of grounds, but the only ground that would have validity for a capitalist is the ground he establishes for himself. Therefore, in judging whether or not capitalism works, I use only the criteria that an intellectually honest capitalist would use for himself. By purely capitalist standards, capitalism does not work and never has.

What, precisely, does a capitalist mean when he says that capitalism works? Simply this: that the capitalist system can provide a relatively stable and prosperous economic order without a lot of government interference in the market. That is to say, capitalism is basically self-regulating and needs no outside force, such as government, to balance supply and demand and ensure prosperity. Now, the Marxist critic might point out that the "prosperity" excludes a large number of people, and the Georgist or the distributist might point out that capitalism depends, contrary to its own theory, on a certain monopolization of land and the other means of production, but the capitalist is likely to reject these critiques. If he is intellectually honest, however, he cannot fail to notice that capitalism has never been a stable economic order without the heavy involvement of the government. And if this system that we pronounce "working" is really one that requires the heavy hand of government for its stability, can we really call it "capitalist" without at least adding some modifier?

The Two Economies

The people who argue that "capitalism works" are the same people who argue that we should have less government interference in the market.

Minimal government involvement is indeed a laudable goal, however, the plain fact of the matter is that capitalism cannot function without government interference. Capitalism relies on an expanded state to balance aggregate supply and demand. Consider this fact: in the period from 1853 to 1953, the economy was in recession or depression fully 40 percent of the time. Since 1953 the economy has been in recession only 15 percent of the time.[1] Consider the following chart,[2] which depicts the American economy in the period from 1900–2006:

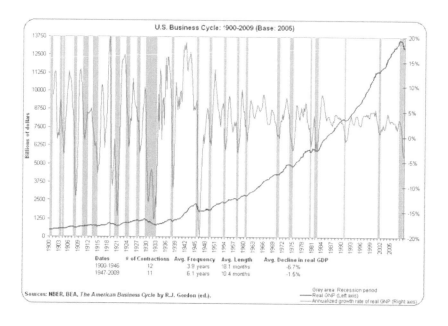

The gray bands represent recessions, the solid line (read on the left-hand scale) represents the quarterly growth rate of the Gross National Product (GNP), and the dotted line (read on the right-hand scale) represents the total GNP in terms of year 2005 dollars.

The first thing we note is that the left side of the chart and the right side seem to indicate two very different economies. The left side is dominated by gray areas, that is, by an amount of economic distress that would simply be politically untenable today, while the right side is mostly white. The solid line on the left side indicates an economy of wild swings, of alternating economic euphoria and depression, while on the right the changes are gentler. Finally, the slope of the dotted line is very shallow on the left side, indicating an economy which cannot sustain growth, and very steep on the right side, indicating an economy where steady growth has become the norm. What distinguishes the right and left sides of this chart, and the two different economies they illustrate, is the introduction of Keynesian economic policies during World War II, policies which have become decisive in all advanced economies, no matter what the ideological bent of the regime in power. Republican or Democrat, liberal or conservative, European or American, they have all followed it for the very simple reason that it works, or at least works well enough to provide for political survival in democratic nations. A politician who actually advanced the policies of the left side of the chart simply would not survive to the next election.

This is not to say that nations haven't tried "left-side" policies. Since the rise of Margaret Thatcher in 1979 and Ronald Reagan in 1980, the political rhetoric has been about "free markets," "lower taxes," and "less government interference." Both Reagan and Thatcher took Friedrich von Hayek as their economic mentor, but the more "Hayekian" the economic rhetoric became, the more Keynesian the economy has actually become. The unintended consequences of Hayek's policies have always been the opposite of what Hayek wanted: larger governments, greater debts, more centralized economic power, and so forth. Keynes's policies may indeed be, as Hayek claimed, a "road to serfdom," but Hayek's policies have turned out to be a super-highway to that same dismal destination. Since the Reagan administration, the World Bank has forced Hayek's economic policies on all the developing economies, and the results have been uniformly dismal. Indeed, the theories of Hayek have been tested just as much as have the theories of Karl Marx, and with about the same results: more government power, less economic freedom. Under neither theory did the state wither away, but rather it became an all-encompassing behemoth. Both Marx and Hayek wished for a "withering away of the state"; both delivered great leaps in government power.

Under the free-market rhetoric of "conservative" regimes, the government has not shrunk, but expanded, so much so that we now have a government of nearly imperial power and privilege, headed by an imperial presidency that ignores not only the laws of Congress and the Constitution, but even basic human "laws" such as the law against torture as an instrument of state policy. Government expenditures as a share of GDP are about the same as they were before the conservative ascendency, but the cost of government has far exceeded its tax base. The result has been an increased dependence on borrowing. At the start of the Reagan administration, the national debt was about $700 billion; at the close of the Reagan-Bush era, it had tripled to $2.1 trillion. It doubled again and then doubled again, and now stands in excess of $12 trillion. This increased debt represents an effective tax increase, since borrowing is taxing too, but a tax *shifted* onto the next generations.

This leads us to an unavoidable conclusion: *capitalism and the free market are incompatible.* History shows, beyond any reasonable doubt, that the growth of capitalism and the growth of government go hand in hand. Capitalism and big government are not, as in the popular imagination and the economic treatises, things opposed; rather, the one grows on the back of the other, and the more you get of one, the more you will need of the other.

Distributists will not be surprised at this result, since it exactly matches the predictions that Belloc made in *The Servile State.* The capitalist state, Belloc believed, would grow increasingly unstable, and could only stabilize itself by enlisting the power of government.[3] Belloc wrote before the rise of Keynes, but Keynes's methods were no surprise to readers of Belloc. Keynes indeed found a "solution," but Belloc had already predicted the solution: servility. It was Keynes's intention to make the citizen freer by freeing him from economic insecurity. But in Keynesian states, people become less free; they cease to be citizens and become mere clients of the state, where even their most ordinary needs are the subject of one or more governmental bureaucracies, and where even ordinary local problems become the responsibility of the most distant levels of government.

We can summarize Keynes's theory as one of a *managed economy.* At the start of a recession, the government would lower taxes and increase spending, thereby running up debts, to increase economic activity. As the economy improves, the government would raise taxes and lower spending to pay off the accumulated debts, and thereby choke off any wasteful booms. Between the two poles, the boom-and-bust cycle would be broken. Governments were more than willing to follow the first part of the prescription, and pile up debts to prevent or lessen recessions. But when it came to the second part, they lacked the will. As the saying goes, nobody wanted to take away the punch bowl just as the party was getting started, or at least nobody who was facing an election campaign. Thus, the debts tend to accumulate, which makes high taxes a *structural* part of the economy; unless a government is willing to default on its debts, it must first pay the interest before any other function of government can be funded. This half-baked Keynesian policy is effective at managing recessions, but isn't normally attempted to manage booms.

As successful as Keynesianism has been at rescuing capitalism from itself, one wonders if this cycle can continue. Each new business cycle seems to require greater intervention than the last, and this latest crisis requires gargantuan efforts. Can this exercise in gigantism continue forever? Most likely not, at least not in a finite world; sooner or later we come to a point where the system can no longer sustain itself. That point may be now. Certainly a $12 trillion debt at the federal level alone is daunting enough, and that debt shows no sign of abating. But even more problematic is the increasingly servile nature of the population, a population easily manipulated by commercial advertising and political spin. The servility which Belloc predicted, which Keynes institutional-ized, and which Hayek feared on the theoretical level but did so much to advance on the practical level, is now upon us. Thus our problem transcends the merely economic; we must deal with a cultural problem as well. We have saddled our children with crushing debts, just as we have deprived them of the independent spirit which leads a man to pay his debts.

The Law of Unintended Consequences

It is somewhat of a mystery why Keynesianism should succeed, after a fashion, where capitalism fails. Neither Keynes nor Hayek intended the kind of government we have nor the kind of servility we see, yet this is what we have. What went wrong? Both theories ran smack-dab into the "law of unintended consequences." This law states that the unintended consequences of our actions are always greater than the intended ones. It is a natural outcome of the fact that we are finite creatures, with incomplete knowledge of the present and no knowledge of the future. The consequences of any action are potentially infinite, while our intentions are always limited. Therefore consequences must always outstrip intentions.

There are further problems when man theorizes about human sys-tems. Man builds theoretical models, but by definition, what a model leaves out is always greater than what it includes. We hope and believe that our models have included all that is important and left out all that is inconsequential. We search for principles which lie at the heart of things, but how are we to know that we have located those principles? In the physical sciences, we can often test our theories in a laboratory; we can strictly control the environment and vary only the factor we wish to test. But this procedure does not work for human systems. How is man to test his economic theories? How is he to know if he has included all the important elements? Let me suggest that we do have a laboratory, and that laboratory is called "history." It is an imperfect laboratory, because we can never control all the variables. Further, there are no raw facts in this lab, but only a series of interpretations we place on actual events. Hence, the reading of the results will always be a discursive and critical enterprise. Nevertheless, when we look at charts like the one in this chapter, what might be called the "lab" results of economic history, we certainly notice some very consistent features on the right and left sides of the chart. Anyone who reads the chart and offers an interpretation must account for the dramatic change in the middle of the chart and for the consistencies on each side of the chart.

When we see an idea fail consistently, and fail in exactly the same way in every case, we can be sure that something essential has been left out of the theory. The greater the unintended consequences, the more confident we are that something is missing. And when we compare the theory with something that historically works better, we attempt to identify the element that is responsible for the difference. In the case of Keynes and Hayek, I believe that the difference is the different position that distributive justice has in each theory.

In the case of Hayek, justice simply isn't an issue; his major concern is with freedom. It is noteworthy that he uses the term "justice" just three times, but "freedom" eighty-seven times.[4] Hayek is continuing one element of the neoclassical tradition in economics, a tradition which had eliminated justice as an economic consideration. It was not that the neoclassicals were opposed to justice; they just didn't regard it as an economic question. The neoclassicals triumphed in economic theory around the turn of the twentieth century. Henceforth, economics would no longer be a moral endeavor, but a "scientific" one. However, the system became increasingly unstable, and teetered on the verge of collapse beginning in 1929. Keynes did his theorizing in the midst of this collapse. Freedom was less of an issue to him, while saving the situation was of primary importance. Keynes's recipe for saving the system was the (re)distribution of wealth and income. He used the term "freedom" only four times, but the term "distribution" fifty-seven times.

The theories of Keynes and Hayek are often presented as opposing theories, but in fact the opposition is more apparent than real. Hayek was not opposed to at least some redistribution, as he noted in *The Road to Serfdom*:

There is no reason why, in a society which has reached the general level of wealth ours has, the first kind of security should not be guaranteed to all without endangering general freedom; that is: some minimum of food, shelter and clothing, sufficient to preserve health. Nor is there any reason why the state should not help to organize a comprehensive system of social insurance in providing for those common hazards of life against which few can make adequate provision.[5]

For his own part, Keynes praised *The Road to Serfdom*:

In my opinion it is a grand book. We all have the greatest reason to be grateful to you for saying so well what needs so much

19

to be said. You will not expect me to accept quite all the economic dicta in it. But morally and philosophically I find myself in agreement with virtually the whole of it; and not only in agreement, but in a deeply moved agreement.[6]

Keynes accepted the neoclassical dictum of a value-free economics; he merely denied that such an economic system could maintain itself in equilibrium for very long, if at all. He felt that such a system led inevitably to great disparities in wealth and income, and that no economy could balance itself in the face of these manifest imbalances. "The outstanding faults of the economic society in which we live," he said, "are its failure to provide for full employment and its arbitrary and inequitable distribution of wealth and incomes."[7]

What Keynes actually proposed was not so much an overturning of the capitalist system, as a neat division of labor: the capitalist system would create wealth, and the political system would redistribute it in sufficient amounts to maintain aggregate demand and keep the economy from collapsing. In other words, Keynes bowed to the abandonment of justice as an *economic* principle, and made it into a purely *political* concern; *distributive* justice became *re-distributive,* not so much a matter for economists as for bureaucrats. Insofar as Keynes had some consideration for distributive justice, economies built on his principles have been able to function. But insofar as they depend on an ever-growing bureaucracy, they are always in danger of consuming themselves.

Hayek opposed Keynes because he believed that Keynes's theory inevitably led to state control of the economy and the attendant loss of freedom. The problem in looking at both of these thinkers is not that either of them is wrong, but rather that both of them are right. With Hayek, we oppose the expansion of state power as a threat to freedom;

with Keynes, we assert the necessity of justice, and not merely on moral ground, but on the practical ground that it is the only way to make an economy work. The problem occurs when their two theories are combined in an incoherent way, as has been the case since the 1980s. What results is not merely a road to serfdom, but a super-highway to that same dismal end. Pure capitalism disappeared in the 1940s, caught in its own contradictions, and Keynesian capitalism now appears mired in unrepayable debts and ever-greater intrusions into the economic and personal lives of its citizens. The Keynesian system is definitely broken, or at least in the process of breaking itself apart, just as the previous system broke itself apart in the 1930s. If this interpretation of economic history is correct, then the time has come to consider some alternatives.

What is needed is not two disjoint and contending theories, but one theory that combines both justice and freedom. The distributive alternative involves invoking the older tradition by recasting economics as the science of *political economy* and reintroducing the question of justice into that science. The next three chapters will take up the crucial question of the status of political economy as a science. In the chapters following the science, we will go into greater detail on the relationship of justice to that science.

3

Political Economy as a Science

Science, Normative and Positive

Someone once remarked that economists suffer from "physics envy." One could certainly make that charge against W. S. Jevons (1835–82), one of the founders of marginal economics, when he wrote that a "perfect system of statistics . . . is the only . . . obstacle in the way of making economics an exact science"; once the statistics have been gathered, the generalization of laws from them "will render economics a science as exact as many of the physical sciences."[1] More than a century has passed since Jevons wrote these words, and in that time there has been a growth of vast bureaucracies, both public and private, devoted to establishing this "perfect system" of statistics. Yet today economics seems no closer to being an exact science than it was in Jevons's day. Despite this failure, economic orthodoxy clings to the notion of itself as a positive science. As Milton Friedman puts it,

Positive economics is in principle independent of any particular ethical position or normative judgments. As [J. M.] Keynes says, it deals with "what is," not with "what ought to be." Its task is to provide a system of generalizations that can be used to make correct predictions about the consequences of any change in circumstances. Its performance is to be judged by the precision, scope, and conformity with experience of the predictions it yields. In short, positive economics is, or can be, an "objective" science, in precisely the same sense as any of the physical sciences.[2]

Underlying Friedman's view are two distinctions: a distinction between *facts* and *values* (the "is" and the "ought to be" of things), and a corresponding distinction between a *normative* science and a *positive* one, with the former reflecting the world of values and the latter the world of facts. So which kind of science is economics, normative or positive?

I will suggest that the question is meaningless. *Every* science, insofar as it really is a science, is *both* positive and normative. Every science, insofar as it is a science, must be "normalized" to some criteria of truth. These truths arise from two sources: an internal and an external source. The internal criteria involve a science's proper subject matter and methodology. But these criteria are insufficient to found any science as a science. In addition, there must be external criteria of truth, and these truths can only come from one or more higher sciences. In the absence of such an external check, the science will merely be circular, dependent on nothing but itself and disconnected from the hierarchy of truth. Thus, for example, biology is responsible to chemistry, chemistry to physics, physics to metaphysics. No biologist can violate the laws of chemistry, and no chemist can reach a conclusion contrary to physics. Thus every science is responsible to its own methodology (and therefore *positive*) and to the higher sciences (and therefore *normative*). Every science has, therefore, both its own proper autonomy,

24

based on its subject matter and methodology, and its own proper connection to the near sciences, based on the hierarchy of truth. In speaking of the autonomy of a science, we should note that it is only a *relative* autonomy, not an absolute one. A scientist's obligation to be faithful to his proper method does not relieve him of the obligation to higher truths. No science can provide its own criteria of truth without being circular. When a science attempts to do so, one of two things happens: Either the science breaks up into mutually warring camps whose disputes can never be resolved because there are no accepted criteria of truth by which to resolve them, or it becomes merely dogmatic permitting no rational examination of its premises. In economics, both things have happened: the science is divided into warring factions with no arbiter of truth among them; the principles of the various factions have become dogmatic statements with little connection to reality.

The Physical and Humane Sciences

The hierarchy of science allows us to define what science is, because science is not a mere collection of facts, nor just free-floating knowledge. Rather, it is knowledge integrated into a hierarchy of truth. To know a thing, anything, it is not sufficient to know the thing in itself; one must know also how it fits with everything else, what its relationships are with the rest of the world. Science, then, is not just knowledge, but organized knowledge. It is precisely this organization that makes it science. We have many other kinds of knowledge, such as tacit or intuitive knowledge, but these are not scientific until they can be integrated into the hierarchy of knowledge, and thereby submit themselves to the tests of truth that come from the higher sciences. Until we know the thing in the fullness of its relationships, we don't really know it at all. Therefore science is not just about describing things in themselves, but about describing things in their full relationships with everything else. Now, everything that exists is related to everything else that exists in one way or another. Nevertheless, we can identify two general hierarchies of knowledge, two great branches of science, the *physical* and the *humane* sciences. The first thing to determine about any science, therefore, is not whether it is normative or positive, but whether it is a physical or a humane science.

The distinction between these two branches of science concerns how the objects of the science are moved to their ends. Physical objects are moved to their ends by laws outside of themselves, such as the law of gravity. They do not exhibit any degrees of freedom. For example, the planets are kept in their orbits by the law of gravity, and no planet can suddenly decide to reverse its course and visit a new region of the heavens. In other words, the motions of physical objects are completely deterministic; they are bound by the laws of nature and cannot deviate from them. We can examine nature and discover its laws, laws that exist independently of will and intention. This examination of nature we may call "naturalism," and these sciences all terminate in physics, the master science for the study of physical objects.

Man, of course, is another physical object in the universe of objects, and is bound by the law of gravity no less than any of the planets. He is also something more, however, because while a planet cannot determine its own course, we *must* determine ours. That is, we are not moved to our ends by a law like gravity, but by the choices we make. Man is that being that can choose his own ends and make judgments about the best means to achieve his ends. This freedom towards ends and means is the essence of what it means to be human. The humane sciences, therefore, have a completely different aim than the physical sciences. The latter aim at discovering the physical laws that must be followed and are always in fact followed; the former aim at discovering laws that *ought* to be followed and detailing the consequences of not following those laws. Humane sciences have the human person for their object, and specifically the human person in relationship, whether that is the relationship a person has with himself, his family, his community, the natural environment, or God. Now, political economy deals with economic relationships, those relationships necessary for the material provisioning of society. It is therefore a humane science and not a physical science. Like all humane sciences, economics is about *right relationships.*

Facts without Values?

At this point, the positivist is likely to object that no one can tell us what kinds of relationships are "right" or "wrong." We can only note the facts and predict the consequences. Therefore science, economic or otherwise, should simply stick to the facts and let the moral chips fall where they may. This view is based on a distinction between facts and values. As D. Stephen Long noted in *Divine Economy: Theology and the Market,* "The fact-value distinction has become so determinative in the modern world that we seldom even recognize the many ways our politics, economics, even our theology assume and perpetuate this distinction."[3] The fact-value distinction actually has its roots in medieval theology. The medieval theologians insisted that the material world reflected the eternal order of God and operated on God-given laws which could be known without any direct reference to theology. This allowed a measure of autonomy for the physical sciences. The distinction was not a real distinction, however, but a methodological one confined to physical motions; the motions of the human will could not so easily be measured and numbered. With the Enlightenment sages, however, the distinction became a real one—an *ontological* distinction—that extended even to human motions. All motions, even human ones, would be reduced to number and quantity and divorced from theology and ethics. As David Hume put it,

> When we run over libraries, persuaded of these principles, what havoc must we make? If we take in our hand any volume; of divinity or school metaphysics, for instance; let us ask, Does it contain any abstract reasoning concerning quantity or number? No. Does it contain any experimental reasoning concerning matter of fact and existence? No. Commit it then to the flames: for it can contain nothing but sophistry and illusion.[4]

This test, known as "Hume's fork," is by now so enshrined in our thinking that it has become traditional, with even Christian economists joining in his book burning without a second thought.

Perhaps the best example of the Christian expression of this distinction comes from Alejandro Chafuen, who posits a distinction in natural law itself between the "analytical" and the "normative." For Chafuen, "ethical considerations . . . have no impact on underlying truths,"[5] and *"no ethical judgment can invalidate an economic law,"*[6] a law arrived at without regard to ethics. However, it is fair to question whether Chafuen (and the moderns in general) have a proper understanding of natural law: Has he merely confused it with naturalism? Can there be a value-free law for humans? The answer to these questions depends on one's theology. The older view of natural law situated it within a discernment of the meanings of things, that is, within their *proper acts* and *ends*. Thus, natural law would always involve a *teleology*, a perception of final meaning. Such perceptions, however, involve philosophical, theological, and cultural questions. The Enlightenment view of nature sought to divorce natural law from any moral or theological authority. Is this actually possible?

Let us take a simple deduction from nature: lions eat lambs, therefore the strong prey on the weak. The conclusion would seem to be an unavoidable deduction from the indubitably factual premise, a pure instance of a natural law, blissfully free of any moral or theological foundation. This apparently simple conclusion, however, contains a hidden assumption: the premise concerns animals, but the conclusion is applied to men. Is this valid? Yes, if man is no more than an animal; no, if man transcends the animals. If the latter is true, then natural law can never be just a reading of nature, but must be guided by a consideration of the end and nature of man. Can the issue be resolved one way or another by an appeal to pure reason? No, because both views rest on a purely theological foundation. Man may or may not be just an advanced animal and nothing more. Certainly, he is an advanced animal, but the status of the "something more" cannot be proved—or disproved. Certainly, both men and lions enjoy a leg of lamb for lunch; quite possibly, speech is no more than an advanced form of roaring or baying. There is simply no "proof" that men transcend, or do not transcend, the animals; it is a matter of faith and faith alone. Therefore, the question of whether the proposition is a valid deduction from nature depends not on the raw facts (which cannot be disputed) but on the theology by which one reads those facts. And this will be true for every statement which purports to be a "value-free" conclusion from the natural world. The only question is whether the values are explicit or hidden; if the latter, men will delude themselves into thinking that their thinking is "value-free," when in fact it is a mere attempt to impose their values on others. The solution is never to proclaim a "value-free" conclusion, but to make the values that underlie the conclusion explicit, thereby exposing them to critique and evaluation.

Even if the fact-value distinction could be maintained, it is not always clear which are the facts and which are the values. For example, if we take the distinction seriously, we must allow the following case:[7] Mrs. Harris is an attorney at the top of her profession who bills her time at $500 an hour. Mr. Harris, on the other hand, is a bit of a lout. He calls her at work demanding a bit of "afternoon delight." Wishing to be a dutiful wife, she considers her options. Since she is not only an attorney, but also understands economics, she believes that her decision ought to turn on the opportunity costs of the alternatives. She can go home for an hour and lose $500, or she can call an escort service to provide a suitable surrogate for $150. Thus she must measure the gain of $350 against the loss of $500 and decide how the "opportunity cost" compares to the relative values of sexual pleasure and infidelity. Now, an economist might say that the "facts" of the case involve the opportunity costs, while the concepts of adultery and fidelity are mere values. But this is not at all clear. The relative prices of lawyers and prostitutes are mere social valuations that change from culture to culture and, indeed, from moment to moment; they seem to lack the ontological grounding that one would expect from a "fact." On the other hand, adultery is a fact which "has much more concrete or empirical reality than the putative economic facts mentioned. We can point to the historical embodiment of something called 'adultery' much more readily than something called 'opportunity cost.'"[8]

It would seem, therefore, that the world of human beings cannot be neatly divided into a realm of facts and a realm of values. While there may be, at certain times and in certain cases, a methodological advantage to making such a distinction, it is merely a way of speaking of things for limited purposes and involves no real ontological distinction. Therefore, Chafuen's case for a division in the natural law seems to have failed. A realm of pure "facticity" in human affairs is doubtful. All human observation requires some theoretical framework to make sense of the mere sense impressions. The theoretical framework always involves some value judgments. For example, in measuring unemployment, Charles Clark notes that,

> The economist must first start by making the decision that
> [unemployment] needs theoretical explanation and second
> [he] must define what unemployment is, both of which are
> blatantly value-laden (and political) activities. Furthermore,
> the choice of what methods to use to investigate this phenom-
> enon also involves value judgments, as does selection of the
> critical criteria about what will be accepted as the "final term"
> in the analysis, the bases of what arguments will or will not
> be accepted. However, values and value judgments enter into
> theory construction on the ground floor by giving the theorist
> the "vision" of the reality s(he) is attempting to explain. This
> "vision" is pre-analytical in the sense that it exists before theo-
> retical activity takes place.[9]

We are, of course, bombarded each day by reams of economic "facts" and statistics. Each and every one of them is surrounded by the same constellation of political and value-laden decisions. This does not make them invalid or useless, but we must understand the value-laden deci-sions that went into making each of these numbers. The numbers are not like the numbers we get from looking at a telescope or some other instrument used in the physical sciences. Rather, each number reflects a judgment about what the purpose and the meaning of economics are.

Humane Science and Teleology

The major division of the sciences, then, is not the normative-positive duality, but a division based on the object of the sciences, whether they are merely physical or fully human. For the physical sciences, we need only examine the physical world to note the relationships and regularities, and we have, in most cases, ample room for discovering laws and testing them empirically. But when we deal with the humane sciences, the task becomes more complex, for a simple examination of persons cannot be undertaken without first determining what a "right" state of affairs ought to be. For example, if we practice medicine, we must have some idea of what good health is; we must have some normative state the departure from which constitutes disease. This seems like a straightforward process in physical medicine (although it is actually fraught with many difficulties and conundrums), but can become somewhat complex when we look at, for instance, psychology. For example, if we take two psychologists, one of whom believes that mental health means giving expression to every sexual impulse, and another who believes that sexuality should mainly be expressed in marriage and family, it is obvious that they will give very different kinds of advice. I have no intention of trying to sort out those issues here; I merely point out that the advice given will depend on each psychologist's perception of what it means to be a human being, on what the ends and purposes of our humanity are.

This is the case with every humane science. Its first task is to understand the ends and purposes of the human person, in all of his or her relationships, and that particular science's role in contributing to those ends and purposes. This search for ends and purposes is called *teleology,* from the Greek *telos,* a word which connotes *that which completes or perfects a thing.* Each humane science begins, as it were, backwards, with the ends of man, whether those are the ends of his physical or mental health, his social order, his political peace, his need to pursue truth and knowledge, etc. Underneath all of these ends there lies the necessity of a certain material sufficiency. Without having some security of food, clothing, and shelter, it is difficult to pursue any of the other ends of man. Now, all of these other ends may be higher than these bare necessities, but every other end presumes the necessities, for no man can long pursue anything else if he cannot get enough to eat. Hence, the pursuit of these ends is basic to the pursuit of every other end, and the more easily they can be obtained, the more time and energy can be devoted to the pursuit of other goals. Now, the political economy is the science which deals with the pursuit of man's material needs, and so it is foundational to every other humane science; even the priest, the philosopher, and the artist need to eat. Therefore, in order to understand the science of political economy, we must ask in greater detail just what the purpose of this science is, which is the topic of our next chapter.

4

The Purpose of an Economy

What Must an Economy Do?

The indispensable requirement for any economic system is that it must provide the material basis for life for a sufficient number of its citizens so that society can continue for another season. In addition, it must provide a sufficient surplus so that society can be repopulated and continue for another generation. If either of these conditions is not met, then society simply disappears and further discussion is unnecessary.

But in addition to the few things that an economy *must* do, there is a longer list of things it *ought* to do. For example, an economy ought to provide the material basis of life for as many members of society as possible, and ideally for all members. It ought to provide for a certain level of material comfort and security; it ought to reward work, ingenuity, thrift, and inventiveness; it ought to supply sufficient excess to fund common goods such as the national defense, religious works, education, etc.; it ought to provide the ground for liberty; it ought to provide the ground for social harmony, that is, each citizen ought to be able to believe that his efforts are fairly rewarded, and that no one lives off of the efforts of another.

The list of things an economy should do implies another list of things it *should not* do. For example, it should not depend on slavery; it should not deprive work (including the "stored-up" work known as "capital") of its just rewards; it should not reward sloth, that is, create wealth not based on some productive endeavor; it must not weaken social bonds or encourage class warfare, and so forth. Taken together, these lists of what an economy *must* do, what it *ought* to do, and what it *ought not* to do, provide us with a set of criteria upon which we may make firm judgments about the success or failure of any particular economy, most particularly our own. Granted, these judgments can never be precise. We can always point to some wealth acquired without work, some work not fairly compensated, some shortfall in the material provisioning of society. What we must really judge, however, is whether these shortcomings are endemic to the society, or merely limited failures, failures which, in an imperfect world, are expected in any system.

The Economic Problem

What is economics? According to economist C. M. A. Clark, "Economics is about social provisioning, or how societies provide for their material reproduction."[1] This definition deals with a more basic problem than do the more common definitions of economics, which generally involve "the allocation of scarce resources among alternate uses." Resources certainly must be allocated, but such definitions leave out the purpose of these allocations. Further, the neoclassical definition biases the conversation in favor of scarcity rather than abundance; but the whole purpose of resource allocations—the whole reason for economizing—is to allow for a relative abundance. It is the means (resources) which may be scarce, but not necessarily the ends. Therefore, the more fundamental economic question involves social provisioning. In answering this question, we must deal with three further questions: What to produce? How to produce it? To whom should the benefits be distributed?

What to produce? What a society produces is a direct reflection of its dominant values, or at least of the values of those who dominate society. It would seem that some things *need* to be produced and are therefore *natural* and beyond cultural considerations. But while things like food, clothing, and shelter are necessary, the form they actually take is always cultural. For example, we must eat to live regardless of what language we speak, but what we actually eat—spaghetti, or egg foo young, or hamburgers—is always a cultural product.

How to produce it? This is a question both of human technology and abilities. There must be a means of assigning tasks, something which normally has a large social content. For example, tasks will be assigned at least partially on the basis of education, but who gets educated and who doesn't is largely a social decision.

To whom should we distribute the product? This question has both discretionary and necessary aspects. Certainly the product must be divided so that enough members of society can subsist and reproduce the next group of workers. Beyond that, distribution has strong discretionary elements. Normally, the actual distributions will depend on the values of the society at large, or perhaps will reflect the values only of the ruling class. The solution is largely a matter of power relationships rather than of some "pure" economics.

Solutions: Tradition, Command, and Market

The answers to the questions of social provisioning can come from three sources: tradition, command, or the market.[2]

Tradition: The past guides the present; what to produce this year is guided by what was produced last year. There is little change and less freedom. All three questions are answered, but answered, as it were, in advance and with little option for growth and change.

Command: Command economies rely on some central authority to provide all the answers. While this ensures that all the questions are answered, the quality of such answers may be open to doubt, especially if the values of the planners are at odds with the values of society at large. The planners could be seeking either the interests of the common good or their own interests. Nevertheless, economies heavily dependent on command have functioned successfully and left behind great monuments such as the pyramids or the medieval cathedrals.

Market: The forces of supply and demand dictate the answers, with each individual responding to price signals in order to maximize utility. In this way, it is believed, the market is self-organizing and capable of creating order out of chaos. But as Charles Clark has noted:

> This is the myth of the market. Markets are not natural phenomenon, but are socially created. In the real world the market mechanism is best at dealing with small changes to an already existing economic order, providing the signaling function of adjusting relative prices so that a small number of market participants can adjust their behavior. Markets, however, cannot generate this order. All markets are social institutions, embedded in particular societies and in history. They have rules of behavior, laws and customs. These come from tradition. Also they have property rights and methods for enforcing these rules and customs. These come from command. Without the proper context, markets are inefficient and chaotic, as Russia is currently demonstrating to the world.[3]

Clearly, markets do not generate order, but are based on a preexisting social order which they then help direct. But they can also help to destroy that order. Indeed, the assumption that all things can be based on self-interest destroys the very basis of virtue which is presumed by the market. A pure market system has never been attempted, because it cannot be attempted. Markets require fully socialized and ethical participants in order to function, but an attempt to establish a pure market system displaces these traditional sources of economic order, that is, families and shared political values. It is no accident that as the force of custom and virtue diminishes, the role of law—and lawyers—increases. So too does the role of politics and bureaucracies. Force, legal or political, must replace the virtues that a "pure" market system helps to undermine.

Economics and the Family

If economics requires fully socialized participants, *and* if economics is about social provisioning, then the question of the family cannot be divorced from economic questions. For economic actors, producers, and consumers are "produced" and socialized within the confines of the family; without the family there will be no next generation, and hence no future, for the economists to worry about. Therefore, it is the family that is the basic economic unit as well as the basic social unit. Modern economics tends to ignore the role of the family completely to focus on the individual. However, the individual, by himself, is sterile and not a self-sustaining entity. Neoclassical economics thus has no way to explain how new workers come into the economy, and hence it has no way to explain growth. John Mueller has characterized these shortcomings in economics as "The Economic Stork Theory." In the stork theory, workers arrive in the economy fully grown, fully trained, and fully socialized. These stork-borne workers are a "given";

that is, there is no way to explain the growth in workers or their level of training and socialization, and hence little reason to support them with political or fiscal policies. Mueller describes the theory as follows:

> I have called this set of assumptions the stork theory, since it implicitly assumes that adult workers spring from out of the blue, as if brought by a large stork: in effect, denying Aristotle's observation that humans are "conjugal" or "matrimonial" animals. Given the stork theory's assumptions, the accumulation of workers' tools—buildings and machines—is the only possible source of economic growth that can be affected by policymakers, and the total tax burden not only should, but inevitably must, fall entirely upon the incomes of workers (who under the same assumption cannot avoid such taxes by having fewer or less educated children, though property owners are assumed to be able to avoid taxes on property income by investing less in property). This empirically false assumption—not sound economic theory—underlies the proposals to abolish taxes on property income that are perennially advocated by a cottage industry of (mostly my fellow Republican) economists centered in Washington, D.C. [4]

It is an oddity of modern economics that it depends on treating the worker as just another commodity (labor) for purposes of pricing that labor, but treats the production cost of that "commodity" as something beyond the price system. If we take any other commodity, say a bar of pig iron, it is assumed that the price must cover the cost of production, maintenance, and depreciation, or the product will be withdrawn from the market. But in regards to labor, this assumption is never examined. For labor has its own "production cost" (the family) and its own "maintenance" costs (subsistence and healthcare) and its own "depreciation" costs (sickness and old age). Labor cannot simply be withdrawn from the market when these requirements are not met. Therefore, labor—and the family—does not even gain the dignity of a bar of pig iron in modern economic theory.

Scarcity, or "Can There Ever Be Enough to Go Around?"

Scarcity is the most obvious and self-evident economic principle because we live in a finite world. Indeed, scarcity is what makes economizing necessary. When ends and means are confused, however, scarcity itself becomes not something self-evident, but something evidently false. Let me illustrate with an anecdote. When I was a boy in New York City, my family lived in an old brownstone apartment on Manhattan's West Side. We did not have a car; nobody on our street did. However, for fifteen cents we could buy a subway token, and for that fee the cultural and recreational wealth of New York City was ours, even as small children. My brother and I loved to go to the American Museum of Natural History to see the great skeleton of *Tyrannosaurus rex* that dominated the lobby, or the great blue whale that hung in the basement. Or we would go to the Metropolitan Museum of Art and see the armor exhibit, with knights in shining armor mounted on steeds covered in steel plate, lances lowered so that, when you entered the room, they looked like they were charging directly at you. Or for the same fee, we could go to the beaches at Coney Island or Far Rockaway. We were indeed men of the world at the age of seven. But mostly, we were independent; we were free. It was a poor neighborhood, but we were rich in cultural and recreational resources. By contrast, my children grew up in an affluent suburb in Texas. Everybody on the street had at least two cars, but my children had very little transportation. The means of transport were not available to them independently, and hence parents and children were bound together in a relationship similar to that of a lord and his chauffeur; both children and parents lost some of their freedom. It was perhaps good that there were so few places to go, and that the major cultural resources were the mall and the movie theater.

In one case, there was a scarcity of means and an abundance of ends, and in the other, an abundance of means and a scarcity of ends. In one case, cars were scarce and transportation abundant, and in the other, cars were abundant and transportation scarce. Properly considered, scarcity should apply to means, not ends. If we reverse the terms, we end up manufacturing our way into scarcity, and an expensive scarcity at that. In place of robust systems designed according to some notion of the common good, we have narrow systems designed from the premises of individualism which always make the ends, transportation in this case, more problematic. And they are even more problematic the more you invest in them: we spend huge sums of public money on systems that limit access rather than expand it. This same pattern of spending ourselves into scarcity can be seen in education, health care, the military, etc. Expenditures for higher education increase while access to college declines, for example. What is lacking is a purpose, a *telos*, that is to say, a vision of the common good, and a proper distribution function informed by that vision.

The Purpose of an Economy

Let us now summarize our conclusions about the purpose of an economy:

- The subject of political economy is the material provisioning of society.

42

- An economic system must answer three questions: What to produce? How to produce it? And to whom do we distribute the output?
- The answers to these questions will come from a combination of tradition, command, and market forces.
- In order to accomplish the material provisioning of society, the economy must provide for the material provision of the family, because the family is the basis of both the social and economic orders; it is the reason for having an economy and the indispensable condition of an economy.
- The economy must provide for a relative abundance of ends using relatively scarce means.
- It must accomplish all of these tasks in ways that advance freedom.

Taken together, these points provide a teleology for the economy; they define the ends and purposes of any actual economy and give us a set of criteria to make reasonable judgments about that economy. These conclusions determine whether or not the economy is fulfilling its proper functions. However, they say nothing about the means by which an economy reaches its natural ends. Now, the primary means by which an economy fulfills its goals is by achieving a balance between supply and demand, a state called equilibrium. There are various paths to achieving this balance, some of them manifestly better than others. These will be the subject of the next chapter.

5

Equilibrium, or
The Tao of Economics

The Magic Chart

Open any standard economics textbook, and before you have gotten too far into it, you will see a chart that looks like this:

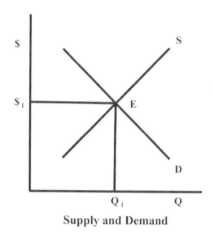

Supply and Demand

The vertical axis represents price for any commodity and the horizontal axis indicates quantity of that commodity. Within the chart there are two lines that cross, "S" for supply and "D" for demand. The supply curve indicates the amount of any commodity that producers are willing to supply at a given price, while the demand curve indicates the amount of that commodity that consumers are willing to buy at a given price. The point where the two lines cross, labeled "E" is called the equilibrium point, while "Q_1" and "$\$_1$" represent the quantity and price at the equilibrium point. The chart is based on an intuitively obvious idea, namely that buyers want to spend as little as they can and suppliers want to get as much as they are able. Hence, the lower the price of something, the more consumers are willing to buy of that product, while the higher the price, the more suppliers are willing to produce. The equilibrium point represents the balance between supply and demand, the point where buyers are willing to buy the exact amount that producers are willing to supply at that price.

This deceptively simple chart is an extremely powerful tool, and economists put it through all sorts of permutations to arrive at all sorts of conclusions. None of that, however, concerns us here; at this point we are mainly interested in understanding the idea of equilibrium, and how societies get to that point. It is no exaggeration to say that the entire structure of modern, neoclassical economics is built on this chart. Therefore, some comments on the chart are in order. The first thing that we must note is that this is an *idealized* representation; it represents equilibrium in a static moment, but an actual economy is dynamic. Prices change from day to day and even from hour to hour. Because it is an idealized portrait, it shows equilibrium as a precise and knowable point that is actually reached. In a real economy—and for any real product—the equilibrium point is rarely known with any precision, but forms an attractor point around which prices and quantities fluctuate. And it should be noted that while we call them "supply" and "demand" curves, they are really both demand curves, since the supply curve represents the producers' demand for money. This would be self-evident in a barter economy. If someone were trading shoes for fish, we would place fish on one axis (it doesn't matter which one) and shoes on the other, and both parties would be simultaneously "demanders" and "suppliers." It is only in a money economy, where goods and services are measured in terms of one special commodity, that we can strictly separate "suppliers" from "demanders." It is important to remember this, because in a money economy, most people become demanders only after first being suppliers, usually by supplying to the market the commodity known as labor.

The Demand Curve

Demand is affected by the consumer's income level, needs, tastes, preferences, the prices of other goods, and his expectations of any changes in price levels. If a consumer's income increases, some portion of the increase will contribute to an overall increase in demand. For example, an increase in the minimum wage might raise overall demand and affect the equilibrium point. What the equilibrium point really measures in not overall demand, but *effective demand,* by which we mean both the desire for the product *and* the ability to pay for it. Note that, in a market system, the equilibrium point will always be less than total demand, usually substantially less. Hence, certain common goods, such as police, schools, or roads are not normally provided as market goods (or some would receive none of them) but as socialized goods.

Needs, tastes, and preferences are often regarded as individual choices, however, the truth is much more complex. While these always appear as personal actions, they are actually socially influenced. In fact, much of what we are has little to do with individual choice. For example, most readers of these words speak English not as an individual choice, but as a social gift; we were given the English language long before we realized that we might have some choice in the matter. Our preferences are heavily influenced by such things as fashion, advertising, workplace dress codes, and social conventions. Even those who wish to escape the conventional most often do so by substituting other conventions. For example, a teenager objecting to conventional styles may adopt "goth" styles, a social subgroup. Examples of a purely individual choice are hard to come by. Economists tend to model demand as the aggregate of purely individual choices, but this may not be the best model of what humans actually do or what we actually are.

Prices of other goods affect demand because we must make choices; to purchase a quantity of commodity A precludes us from using the same money to purchase commodity B. Further, many products have *substitutes*. For example, if the price of beef increases relative to the price of pork, many people will substitute pork for beef in their diets. Hence, a producer competes not only against others producing the same product, but also against those producing products that can be substituted for his.

Another thing we may note about demand is its *elasticity*. Elasticity measures how much change in price is required to change the volume purchased. Some products are highly elastic; a small change in price will lead to large increases or decreases in what is purchased. Other products are inelastic; it takes a large change in price to change buying behavior. For example, most of us must use a certain amount of gasoline to get to work, and have difficulty finding an alternate means of transportation. Therefore, we are likely to pay whatever the market demands for gas, making gas an inelastic commodity.

The idea that as a commodity's price falls people will tend to purchase more of that commodity is the law of demand. It is not, however, a law in the way that gravity is a law, always and everywhere operative.

Rather, it is a tendency, and as such there are many exceptions. Some products actually depend on the price being unreasonably high. A Ford automobile will get you where you are going as well as will a Jaguar, but a Jaguar will display your wealth along the way. If the price of Jaguars were lowered to that of Fords, it is likely they would, after a time, sell less of them, not more. A more common example is athletic shoes. A $130 pair of Nikes may not be any better than the $30 no-name pair that comes out of the same shoe factory in Vietnam. But by placing the "swoosh" on the shoe, the seller can get a large premium, a premium which contributes to the product's image and exclusivity. Again, if he lowered the price to $30, there would be nothing to distinguish it, and sales might actually fall. Nevertheless, and even with all these caveats, the law of demand is still a useful concept, even if it isn't really a law.

Taking all these things together, we note that the deceptively simple demand curve encodes a tremendous amount of information. Any change in the factors making up the demand curve can have large consequences on the shape of the curve and hence on the equilibrium point. Moreover, this encoded information is largely social. Our actions are influenced by others and, in turn, influence others. For example, when we choose to buy a giant Hummer, we increase the demand for gasoline, and thus affect the price that everyone else pays for it, even those who have no interest in monster-sized cars.

The Supply Curve

As complex as the demand curve is, the supply curve presents even more challenges. In the standard, neoclassical theory of economics, it is relatively straightforward: firms supply product to the market until marginal revenue equals marginal costs; this is called *marginal cost pricing*. "Marginal" here means the cost or revenue for the last unit produced. Marginal revenue is simply the price of the product. Marginal cost, however, is highly complex. In general, we know that with a given amount of equipment and labor, we can produce one more unit of a product for a low additional cost, up to a point. Beyond that point, costs per unit will actually start to rise. It will cost more to make the last unit than the product actually sells for; hence, there is no reason to produce past this point. Firms will produce product up to the point that marginal costs equal marginal revenues. Under conditions of perfect competition, this will provide the greatest possible amount of goods to the market at the lowest practical price. Society will benefit, and the firm will make a reasonable, but not outrageous, profit.

The theory is sound; however, actual practice diverges from this theory more often than not. In the first place, knowing the "marginal revenue" means knowing what the demand curve will be, and this is generally just a guess, for all the reasons we have already mentioned. But it is the marginal cost that is most problematic. When an economist thinks of costs, he thinks of all the resources that were consumed in making the product. The businessman, however, only thinks of the costs he actually has to pay. Other costs may be *externalized,* that is, placed upon third parties who are not necessarily purchasers of the product. For example, the owners may get the government to build them roads, finance their facilities, pay part of their work force (with food stamps or housing vouchers, for example), give them tax rebates, etc. The most obvious example of an externalized cost is pollution. A manufacturing process may dump highly toxic chemicals into the air, the land, or the water, causing health problems for everybody else. This is a real cost, but one that does not show up in the business owner's calculations. But even considering just internal costs, these turn out to be complex and difficult to measure, and few companies actually undertake such an analysis. Rather, they depend on strategies other than marginal cost pricing.

If a company has a patent on a product for which there are no substitutes, it may engage in *monopoly pricing*. This is especially the case in the drug industry, where patent protection allows the drug companies to charge tens or even hundreds of dollars for a pill that may cost pennies to manufacture, even considering research costs. If there are a few companies in the same business, they may engage in a similar practice, *oligopoly pricing*. They may use *package pricing*, relying on the reputation or packaging of the product to obtain a higher price, as in the Nike example above. Or they may use *predatory pricing* to price the product below cost and force a weaker competitor out of business. Or, they may use *discrimination pricing*, which sells the same product to different markets at different prices. For example, the same seat on an airplane may cost a different amount depending upon whether the passenger is a business traveler, a leisure traveler, bought the ticket the day of flight or three weeks in advance, is staying over a weekend, etc. These and many other pricing strategies are a long distance from the marginal cost pricing of the standard theory.

Having drawn all of these caveats around the supply and demand curves, have we not then shown that the "Magic Chart" is not really valid? Perhaps, but I don't think so. All we have shown is that the standard tools of neoclassical analysis may not be the best way to understand equilibrium. The theoretical model may be insufficiently "scientific," that is, not well related to the way things really work. The truth is that all successful economies reach equilibrium, more or less. But the problem (and the analytical challenge) comes in the fact that they reach it through both economic and noneconomic means. It is the means by which equilibrium is reached that must be correctly analyzed.

Economic Equilibrium

When people come together in families or firms to produce things, they add wealth to the economy; in fact, this is the only economic way to add wealth.[1] If they get an equitable share of the output, or the wealth they create, there will be enough purchasing power in the economy to buy all the things they produce. This is the much-maligned Say's law of markets, which states that "supply creates its own demand." When there is an excess of goods supplied to the economy, we have a recession, or worse. Say's law is often criticized because, if you examine it closely, it holds that recessions are impossible; there will always be enough purchasing power to clear the markets. Clearly, we purchase things in terms of other things. If, for example, you are a fisherman and you want shoes, you catch fish and trade them with the cobbler (in a barter economy). The total number of things created equals the total number of things that can be used for purchasing the other things. The two quantities are, in fact, the same quantity, so that there can never be a shortage of purchasing power in the economy. Granted, there may be a temporary disequilibrium in any particular market. The fisherman may catch more fish than people really want to eat; the cobbler may make too few shoes. But such a situation will normally not persist. A fisherman who cannot sell all of his fish will cut back on the time spent fishing and devote himself to other things; perhaps leisure, or perhaps he will take up cobbling, thereby adding to the supply of shoes. But in any case, a recession in these circumstances cannot be of long duration or great importance. And yet, recessions *do* happen, quite obviously. Long ones. Deep ones. Serious ones. So what is wrong with Say's law?

To understand the problem, we have to look at the sources of demand in a money economy. These sources are twofold: wages, and interest or profit.[2] Wages are, of course, the rewards of labor, and profit the reward of capital. In another sense, however, these are the same rewards since capital is merely "stored-up" labor, or things produced in one period to be used to continue production in the next period. For example, if a farmer wishes to have a crop next year, he must save some seed corn from this year's crop. Now, the corn he consumes and the corn he saves are the same corn from the same crop. But by saving some corn for seed, it becomes "capital." Hence, the return on this capital is really a return on his prior-period labor, just as his wages are a return to current-period labor. Clearly the returns to capital and labor, interest and wages, spring from the same source (labor). Capital, then, ought to have roughly the same rewards as labor, plus some premium for saving. Or, to use the nomenclature, the returns to capital and labor should be "normalized" to each other. This normalization of incomes from capital and labor is the condition of *equity* in an economy. That is, the same kind and quality of labor, whether in its original or "stored-up" form of capital, should produce roughly the same return.

Interest (or profit) and labor constitute the economic sources of demand, and if they are normalized to each other, economic recessions are unlikely.[3] There will be enough purchasing power distributed equitably to clear the markets. In capitalist economies, the vast majority of men are not capitalists; that is, they do not have sufficient capital to make their own livings, either alone or in cooperation with their neighbors, but must work for wages in order to live. And since the vast majority of men and women work for wages, then the vast majority of goods will have to be distributed through wages. In conditions of equity, this will not be a problem; so long as there is equity, there is likely to be equilibrium, and periods of disequilibrium are likely to be brief. But it may happen, and quite often does, that interest and wages are *not* normalized to each other. In almost all cases (although there are exceptions), this means that capital gets an inordinate share of the rewards of production. Since there are usually fewer capitalists than workers, this means that purchasing power is concentrated into the hands of a few, not spread among the many. This translates to an overall decrease in purchasing power, since the few cannot eat as many Big Macs or wear as many Nikes as the many. This, in turn, means that the vast majority of men and women will not have sufficient purchasing power to clear the markets, and the result will be a disequilibrium condition, that is, a recession.

Some might object at this point that distributions can't matter; even if the CEO gets a great deal more, there will still be the same amount of purchasing power in the economy. This is true—up to a point. But when the disparities become too great, purchasing power disappears. A very few wealthy men simply cannot spend as efficiently as a large mass of poorer men. The CEO may make five hundred times what the line worker makes, but he cannot wear five hundred times the pairs of shoes, eat five hundred times the amount of food, or live in a five hundred bedroom mansion. Of course, he will want to invest the excess, but the very accumulation of money at the top both narrows the market upon which good investment opportunities depend, while providing for an oversupply of capital. This is called the *investor's dilemma,* and we will return to this in an later chapter.

When this happens, governments and societies often look to noneconomic ways of restoring equilibrium.

Noneconomic Equilibrium

The major noneconomic means of restoring equilibrium are charity, welfare and government spending, and consumer credit (usury). Each of these methods transfers purchasing power from one group, which presumably has an excess, to another which has a deficit. The first method, charity, will always be necessary to some degree. This is because even in the most equitable and well-run economies, there will always be people who are incapable of making a decent living, perhaps because of mental impairment, moral deficiency, or physical handicap. One hopes that there is enough generosity and benevolence in society to voluntarily cover the needs of these people. When low wages become widespread and self-interest becomes the dominant motivation in society, however, it is likely that charity will be insufficient, and other means must be used.

The second noneconomic means of equilibrium is welfare, and government spending in general. By these means, the government seeks to reestablish equilibrium conditions either by supplementing the income of some portion of the population, or simply by increasing its spending to create more jobs and thus add more purchasing power to the economy. This strategy is at the heart of Keynesian economics. The "market" economy is allowed to continue to produce inequitable conditions, but the government will tax and redistribute the excess incomes in an amount sufficient to restore equilibrium. For a while, this method worked fairly well; however, it created some problems. In the first place, it created entitlements. Unlike charity, which depends on the benevolence of the donors and may evoke gratitude on the part of the recipients, welfare depends on the police powers of government and is more likely to evoke resentment on the part of both the recipients and the "donors." Further, these redistributions require increasingly intrusive bureaucracies to collect and disburse the funds. The recipients, no less than the donors, find that every aspect of their life is subject to government review and control, and this is never a comfortable feeling for either party.

Despite the fact that Keynesian transfers now consume a huge portion of the federal and state budgets, these transfers have been, for some years now, insufficient to balance supply and demand, and for some time now the economy has depended chiefly on the third method, usury or consumer credit. Here we must distinguish between lending for investment and usury. Investment means giving money to firms and entrepreneurs in order to expand production and increase the wealth of society. In this case, interest is merely the investor's participation in the profits; it is the "wage" of the capital supplied, and the one who supplies it is entitled in justice to that wage. Usury, on the other hand, is lending money at interest to increase consumption. Nothing is added to the wealth of society, however much may be added to the wealth of the lender. Since nothing is produced, there is no valid claim to profit. Interest payments in this case merely constitute a transfer of wealth from the borrower to the lender, but no net increase in the social stock of wealth. In fact, wealth is actually "used up" in this process without making a contribution to production, hence the name "usury."

This is the plastic economy, an economy based on credit cards. To the extent that an economy depends on consumer credit, it is, quite literally, a house of cards, and will be as unstable as those structures usually are. In fact, usury is the most destructive way of increasing demand. Usury actually delays the problem, postpones the crisis to a future period. This is because a borrowed dollar used to increase demand today must be paid back tomorrow and hence will decrease demand in a future period by that same dollar—plus interest. This requires more borrowing, which of course only makes the problem worse. Eventually, the system falls of its own weight, as credit is extended to an increasingly weakened consumer, and a credit crisis results.

Noneconomic equilibrium provides us with a measure of just how well an economy is doing in *economic* terms. If the economy has a high dependence on noneconomic means, we may assume that there are serious problems in the economy itself. This is an important point.

Those who wish to scale back the extent of government involvement in the economy must first analyze the failures in the economy that make heavy government involvement necessary. Those who would propose a cure, must first analyze the cause. And the cause is always and everywhere the same: a lack of justice.

6

Justice and the Political Economy

T he notion that justice should be a part of the science of economics
is one that many economists resist. They find it problematic to
include a purely moral consideration in a "scientific" discussion such
as economics. They are certainly right that economics is a science, an
organized body of true knowledge. They are wrong, however, to exclude
justice as part of that science, for reasons already covered in chapter
3. Further, in introducing the question of justice we are not innovat-
ing. Justice was part and parcel of economic science from Aristotle
through Aquinas in the Middle Ages and into the Scholastic School
of Salamanca in the seventeenth century. Indeed, economics was no
more than a colony of ethics, and hardly any philosopher or theologian
worth his stipend was without at least some commentary on economics. In the sixteenth century, however, as new forms of ownership and
production began to take hold, a more individualistic approach to economics gradually developed. The ethical framework of medieval economics came under attack, but there was little to replace it. Or rather,
what sought to replace it was a new concept which preached quite

openly that "greed is good." This idea was most famously expressed in Bernard de Mandeville's *The Fable of the Bees: or Private Vices, Publick Benefits* (1724). In *History of Economic Thought,* economist E. K. Hunt summarized Mandeville's position: "He put forth the seemingly strange paradox that the vices most despised in the older moral code . . . would result in the greatest public good."[1] Since Mandeville's day, the entire economic question has centered on the miraculous transformation of "the water of 'self-interest' into a wine of public interest," as R. W. Faulhaber put it.[2]

However, this miracle really isn't possible. Vice—even profitable vice—cannot be made virtuous and hence cannot be the foundation of either public order or sound economics. Indeed, even the most "positivist" economists still retain a residual notion of justice. To be more precise, they marginalize justice and take one kind of justice (justice in exchange) to stand for—and displace—the other kind of justice, distributive justice. In other words, they use just half of justice and so come up with half a theory. But if political economy is to be a science, it must root itself in the whole of justice. And if we are to have a scientific economics, we must start with an understanding of the fullness of justice.

Aristotle's Justice

The reflection on the relationship of justice to economics begins with Aristotle. For Aristotle, justice is not just a part of virtue, but, as he describes in *Nicomachean Ethics,* justice is "virtue entire, nor is the contrary injustice a part of vice, but vice entire."[3] Justice underlies all the virtues and governs all social relations:

And therefore justice is often thought to be the greatest of virtues, and "neither evening nor morning star" is so wonderful;

and proverbially "in justice is every virtue comprehended." And it is complete virtue in its fullest sense, because it is the actual exercise of complete virtue. It is complete because he who possesses it can exercise his virtue not only in himself, but towards his neighbor also.[4]

It is within this relationship of man to man, that is, within justice, that Aristotle locates economics. He presents a sophisticated analysis that includes a demand function, a distinction between use and exchange values, the function of money as the medium between value and demand (or "need"), and usury, among other things. Aristotle begins his reflection with the family, for "[t]he family is the association established by nature for the supply of men's everyday wants."[5] It is the family, and not the individual, that is the starting point (contrary to modern economics) because only the family is self-sufficient; an individual in isolation can neither reproduce nor provide for himself.[6] Man, for Aristotle, is a social being always using language and reason, and always embedded in a cultural milieu governed by justice, which is understood in two senses: distributive and corrective justice.

Distributive justice deals with how society distributes its "common goods." Aristotle defines this as "things that fall to be divided among those who have a share in the constitution."[7] This refers to the common goods of a state, a partnership, or some cooperative enterprise. For Aristotle, these things should be divided by "merit" based on contributions, but what constitutes this merit will be a matter that is determined culturally. Aristotle says, "For democrats identify it [merit] with the status of freeman, supporters of oligarchy with wealth (or with noble birth), and supporters of aristocracy with excellence."[8] This is to say that different societies value individual contributions differently. Some reward power more than ability, and some the reverse. Every society places different values on different kinds of abilities. This means that there is no "value" apart from culture; the measure of individual contributions to the creation of wealth will never be a mathematical formula, but a cultural judgment.

Corrective justice, on the other hand, deals with "justice in exchange"; that is, with transactions between individual men.[9] In this case, justice consists in exchanging equal values, in "having an equal amount before and after the transaction."[10] The problem is how to determine what values are equal when dealing with dissimilar products, which is nearly always the case. To use Aristotle's example: how many pairs of shoes are equal to one house? The only way to know this is by "need," which many economists understand as the demand function mediated by money. Thus the demand for houses and shoes can be compared by looking at their prices and the two can be equated in terms of money. Money, however, is a social convention, as Aristotle notes: "This is why it has the name money (*nomisma*)—because it exists not by nature but by law (*nomos*)."[11] Thus the requirement for equality in exchange comes from the natural law, but the method of implementing it is legal or conventional.

Distributive justice, then, is a distribution of the products of a group distributed to the members of the group, while corrective justice deals with exchanges between individuals. Distributive justice will be proportional to one's contribution to the group, and hence there can be unequal distributions based on unequal contributions. Corrective justice, on the other hand, will always involve equal amounts, like for like. We can note here that the two species of justice will lend themselves to different types of calculations. Corrective justice deals with the equality of thing and thing, mediated by a third thing (money). Thus, it forms a kind of three-body problem and will be subject, at least in principle, to the kinds of complex calculations used in multi-body problems. Distributive justice, on the other hand, involves a judgment of relative merit. This judgment cannot be reduced to a calculation.

Note here that distributive justice refers mainly to the production process, while corrective justice refers mainly to exchanges between individuals or firms. Thus a complete view of justice involves both distributive and corrective aspects, just as a complete view of any economy involves both the production of goods and their exchange. In Aristotle's view of economic systems, the cobbler or the carpenter each gets a proportionate share of the shoes or furniture that his firm produces, a share based on the contribution that he makes. But since no one needs just shoes or furniture, the cobbler and the carpenter exchange these things with each other to correct the imbalance. Of course, cobblers and carpenters, and most other workers, are paid in money rather than goods, but this does not change the underlying theory.

This difference in the types of judgments used in calculating distributive and corrective justice goes a long way toward explaining why neoclassical economics has avoided the subject of distributive justice. Neoclassicism's mathematical bias makes distributive justice problematic and forces unwanted social and cultural elements into the "calculations," elements that cannot, in fact, be mathematically calculated. But since distributive justice deals with production, how can neoclassical economics eliminate distributive justice without also depriving itself of a theory of production? The neoclassical economists get around this by modeling the production process as a series of exchanges, originating in some exchange with nature on the farm, the fishing fleet, or in the mines, and culminating in the exchange with the final consumer of the product. Along the way, labor and capital are exchanged as the product is improved and refined. The problem with this is that mere exchange does not improve any product. To understand this objection, we will have to take a closer look at the processes of exchange and production.

The Exchange Process

Aristotle asserts that corrective justice consists in an arithmetic equality, that is, in "having an equal amount before and after the transaction." This is no more than the commonsense notion of getting a dollar's worth for every dollar spent, of getting your money's worth. But this immediately confronts us with a problem. For if only equal values are exchanged (barring fraud), what is the point or profit in exchange? The short answer is that there is none; exchange merely corrects imbalances in what we own, exchanging what we don't need for what we do. The long answer is that exchange always involves a difference in two values that each commodity has: its *use-value* and its *exchange-value*. The exchange-value is simply the price we have to pay for something; the use-value is our perception of the item's value to us. Normally, we only trade when we perceive that the use-value of an item is higher than its exchange-value for the things we buy, and when the use-value is lower than the exchange-value for the things we sell.

As an example, suppose I am a farmer with $100,000 worth of wheat in my barn, and you are a baker with $100,000 in cash but no wheat. If you had the wheat, you could bake it into bread worth $125,000 plus all your other costs. Hence, the use-value of the wheat is $125,000 to you. To me, however, the use-value of the wheat is nil; I can't eat that much wheat and it costs me to keep it in storage. Therefore, my use-value is lower than the exchange-value, and I am more than willing to sell it. For your part, the use-value is higher than the exchange-value, and you are more than willing to buy it. Hence the trade takes place. Note I can only charge the exchange-value, not the use-value. If, knowing the use-value to the baker, I try to charge you the use-value, you will not buy it, because there is no excess use-value, and you will give me precise instructions on what I can do with my wheat. Even if I happen to have a monopoly on all the wheat in this area (perhaps because a friendly congressman has arranged for me to have an exclusive license) I still would not be able to charge you the full use-value. I may be able to claim a larger share of the use-value, charging you, perhaps, $110,000 or $115,000. But I will still have to leave some gap in order to induce you to make the trade.

The gap between the use-value and the exchange-value of an item is the precise measure of the wealth created by that item. For example, the computer creates such tremendous wealth because its costs are so low relative to its uses. Even a modestly priced computer can give tremendous use-values in terms of business, convenience, and entertainment. Let's take the case of an entrepreneur who is able to combine a modestly priced computer (say, $1,000) and his own labor to run a business that brings in $50,000 plus all other expenses. In this case, the gap is $49,000, which is a large return on a small investment. But suppose the computer cost not $1,000, but $10,000. In this case, the return would only be $40,000, still a good return, but fewer people would be able to use the computer to create new wealth. As the exchange price rises, the exchange-value/use-value gap is narrowed, less wealth is created, and fewer people are able to take advantage of what use-values remain.

The Production Process

Note that the exchange does not create wealth; that happens in the production process. The exchange process merely gives us a measure of the wealth created. Wealth is only created when we change the form or the location of some item. We change a tree into a chair, or relocate carrots from the farm to the grocery store. Each of these increases the use-value of the tree or the carrot, because it is easier to sit in chairs than in trees (even if they can be grown in our living room) and easier to get the carrot when it is in the store than when it is in the ground. In both cases, it is the application of human labor (whether physical or mental) that creates the new value. And this is always the case. Values are created only from human labor applied to the gifts of nature. There is nothing else.

Now, the entrepreneur is raising his hand to point to two other factors: capital and land. But capital also regresses to labor and nature. The only difference between an item of "capital" and a "consumer" product is that the latter is consumed immediately while the former is consumed in the production of new goods. But the process that forms them both is the same. Land is a somewhat different case. It is also made productive only by human labor, and hence resembles capital in this aspect. Land, however, unlike labor and capital, is not consumed in the process of production, nor can it be "manufactured." If I build a factory on a plot of land, it might have a thirty- or forty-year useful life. At the end of that time, the factory is torn down, but the land remains, as good as new and ready for the next use. The labor and the capital that made the factory are gone, but the land remains. This has some implications for political economy which will be addressed in later chapters. For now, the point is that the production process reduces to nature and labor.

Modern economics, in its neoclassical or Austrian forms, attempts to reduce all economic calculation to commutations, that is, exchanges. But mere exchanges, even in accord with corrective justice, cannot account for production. Commutations are merely an exchange of ownership of commodities that already exist, such as when we exchange money for bread. But in the process of production, we deal with something that was not there before. When we take a tree and make chairs, we bring something new into being. In this case, a principle that deals only with changes in ownership will not be sufficient. The problem of distributing the new chairs among the factors that had a hand in their creation can only be solved by distributive justice, by definition. Now this leads us to a rather amazing conclusion: *modern economic science, the science of production and exchange, lacks a coherent production function!*

Again, the economist will counter that he does indeed have a production function, and one that involves a high level of sophisticated mathematics. The function purports that the inputs of capital and labor to production are rewarded according to their actual contribution to the process of production. But in fact, the function assumes what it ought to calculate, namely what share of the production should go to each factor of production, i.e., its price. But instead, the function uses the market price as an input for each factor; that is, it uses as an input what should be an output. It is an example of circular reasoning.

The economists are forced to use this because they are trying to calculate a quantity that simply does not exist, namely, the "independent" contribution of capital and labor to production. Such independent contributions do not exist, at least not in a way that can be calculated, because all production is a *social process,* and apart from each other, and from a particular configuration of factors, no factor has any productivity whatsoever. To illustrate this point, take the example of a football team. A quarterback who can throw a ball a long distance with high accuracy under great pressure certainly makes a big contribution to his team. His individual contribution, however, cannot be figured just from looking at his statistics. If, for example, you were to replace all his 250-pound linemen with 175-pound weaklings, he would spend a good deal of the game introducing himself to the opposing linebackers. His contribution is not independent of the other "factors of production" on the team. A manager who allocated all his personnel funds to the quarterback and left little for the line would lose both line and quarterback. A sensible manager has to make a *judgment* about the relative importance of each position on the team and allocate his funds accordingly. This judgment is guided by the statistics, but is never reducible to them. There are indeed individual contributions to the team, but their worth can only be judged in relation to the particular configuration of talents on that team.

Therefore, economic science, lacking a coherent notion of distributive justice, is not, and cannot be, a complete description of any actual economy. Hence, we are not surprised to learn that 90 percent of economists missed the coming of the current disaster, and the few who did note it were marginalized and ridiculed. Further, we can note that 90 percent missed the last train wreck, and the wreck before that, etc. Clearly, you cannot accurately predict the behavior of a system you cannot accurately describe.

Justice and Economic Efficiency

If wealth is the gap between use-values and exchange-values, then it follows that more wealth is created when exchange-values are kept as low as possible. The lowest possible value for any commodity, over any appreciable length of time, is its cost of production. The cost of production reduces to labor costs, including the cost of the "stored-up" labor known as capital. Therefore, economic efficiency consists in driving price to production costs. Further, we must note here that costs include not just the private costs that a firm incurs, but also the externalized costs, such as the pollution that a particular production process causes.

This definition of economic efficiency immediately presents us with a question: If efficiency consists in driving prices to costs, and if all costs are ultimately labor costs, does it not follow that economic efficiency consists in driving labor costs to their lowest possible level, that is, subsistence? Or to take a practical case, when we outsource the production of shirts or shoes from a high-cost location, such as North Carolina, to a low-cost location, such as Bangladesh, are we not adding to the efficiency of the economy? The answer is that this is the wrong question. The right question is not about "high-cost" or "low-cost," but about "right-cost," by which we mean the cost that is in accord with distributive justice. That is, in order for the economy to achieve equilibrium, both forms of labor—capital and actual labor—must get their proportionate share of the product. If we consider both wages and profit as the just rewards of different kinds of labor, then the labor bill will always be the same, no matter what. But without distributive justice, one form of labor (usually capital) will be overcompensated and the other (actual labor) will be under-compensated. This creates an instant imbalance in the economy leading to an oversupply of capital and a shortage of aggregate demand. In such cases, the economy cannot achieve economic equilibrium and must resort to the noneconomic means mentioned in the last chapter. Unless wages and profits are normalized to each other, the economy cannot be balanced, and the government must step in to prevent collapse. There is no point in complaining about "government interference" in the economy, without addressing the root cause of that interference, which is the failure of the economy to balance itself by economic means alone.

We normally depend on the competitive market to ensure that the maximum amount of goods is provided at the lowest economic price. And when we are speaking of pure commodities, this generally works pretty well, under certain circumstances. These circumstances include a perfectly free market in which production is divided among a large number of small firms. It is somewhat surprising to find how infrequently these conditions are actually met. Most production is controlled by large corporate collectives, each of which has both enormous pricing power and enormous political power. In fact, corporate capitalism may have collectivized production more effectively than any Stalinist bureaucrat could have dreamed of. Further, we have already noted the problem of the externalities, which, by definition, cannot be handled within any market-price system. Finally, we note that the reduction of the production process to an exchange process means that everything used in production must be modeled as a commodity whose price and supply is regulated by the laws of supply and demand. However, there are factors of production which are *not* commodities, which are *not* produced for the market, and whose quantity and price are *not* regulated by the laws of supply and demand. These are the so-called fictitious commodities of land, labor, and money.[12] They escape the logic of exchange, even though no exchange can take place without them. This is of sufficient importance that it will be the subject of the next chapter.

7

The Fictitious Commodities:
Money

L et us review the chart we saw in chapter 5. This chart shows how a
free market balances supply and demand for any commodity, supplying the greatest amount of that commodity for the lowest practical
price, by which we mean the price that will cover all the costs of production *and* eliminate economic rent, that is, a profit higher than necessary
to attract capital to that market. Thus, in theory, the free market will be
the most economically efficient market possible. Of course, this chart

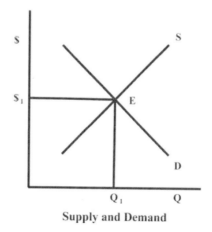

Supply and Demand

represents an ideal, and we have already pointed out various pricing strategies that producers can use to collect an economic rent, that is, to defeat the chart. Nevertheless, it is a marvelous model, and where producers have no pricing power—and thus must take whatever the market gives them—it works very well indeed. However, we need to note that this model applies only to *commodities,* that is, reproducible, elastic objects and services that are made mainly to be exchanged in the marketplace.

Obviously, many things do not fall under the category of a commodity in that sense. The supply of rare wines and fine paintings is not affected by the price. Even when a Monet fetches $30 million, Mr. Monet will not supply the market with any new pictures. Now, the importance of Monets to the market is not very great, and we can ignore the impact, no matter how high the price. But there are three things of great importance to the market, which also have no equilibrium point; these things are money, nature, and man. Their price and quantity are not regulated by supply and demand, and they are not "manufactured" for the market. It may seem strange to say that of money (more about which in a moment) but clearly nature and man are prior to any markets. Neoclassical theory "commodifies" these by reducing nature to land and man to labor. But surely this is mere pretense; land is merely nature subdivided, while labor does not exist apart from the laborer.[1] Land and persons have values other than market values, and when they are reduced to commodities, these other values get externalized. We will address the problems of commodifying labor and nature in the next few chapters, but here we are concerned with money.

Credit and Equilibrium

It may sound strange to say that money is not a commodity, since money (unlike man and nature) has no meaning apart from the market. Nevertheless, it is clear that money is not made to be traded (although there is an incidental trade in currencies), but to serve as a medium of trade. That is, money, like nature and man, is prior to the market, not a result of it. It is true that you can have a market without money, that is, a barter economy, but such a market will be haphazard at best. This is because all trade depends on a *double coincidence.* If I am a fisherman who wants shoes, I will take my fish to the market and hope to find somebody who has shoes but wants fish. In a barter economy, this is a chancy proposition at best. But money solves the problem; we may assume that there is always someone with money who wants our product and always somebody with the product we want who wants our money. Thus, the double coincidence always takes place.

One test for whether something is a real commodity is whether we can draw a "normal" supply and demand chart. Here we look at the market for credit. In standard economic theory, credit is a commodity like

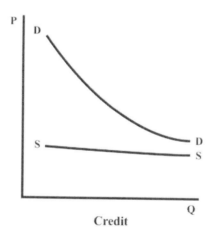

Credit

any other. The "price" of credit is the interest rate, and the interest rate adjusts supply and demand, just as in any other market. However, this is not correct. It is correct that as the price of credit, the interest rate, rises, the demand for credit falls, just as with any real commodity. However, *so does the supply!* The supply and demand curves for credit do not cross (as in the chart). The demand curve looks like any other, but not the supply curve. Note how this chart varies from the standard supply and demand curve: the lines never cross, and there is no equilibrium point.

Why does the supply decline with the increase in the price? Because credit is not "sold," it is allocated by a bureaucratic process. Commodities are sold; anyone with the money may buy them, and the shopkeeper does not examine your credit or your planned use of the commodity. Bankers, on the other hand, lend only to those who are likely to pay them back, and this involves a judgment on the part of the loan officer. He examines both the credit history and the uses of the borrowed funds to determine if the bank is likely to get its money back. When interest rates are low, the bank has a lot of borrowers to choose from. But as the interest rate rises, the most reliable borrowers tend to exit the market. They rely on other sources or simply wait until credit conditions improve. The remaining borrowers are mostly those with weaker credit and less secure business plans. Hence the banks are more reluctant to lend the money and the supply declines along with the demand, the exact opposite of what happens in commodity markets. Shortages of credit are never about a shortage of money, but about a shortage of good uses for the money at the prevailing interest rate. Hence, there is no market-clearing price, nor is there any alternative to the administrative allocation of credit. Therefore, one of the foundations of neoclassical economics collapses both in the theory and in practice.

What Is Money?

The function of money is to serve as a *medium of exchange.* It is vitally important to understand that *money is not wealth,* and it is a grave mistake to confuse it with wealth. Wealth is the actual goods that we have and services we can command. Money is a claim on the *circulating wealth,* that is, the goods and services that are for sale at any given moment. A person with a dollar in his pocket can claim a dollar's worth of the goods and services that are for sale. Hence, another way to think of money is as an accounting method. The money you have in your pocket or your bank account represents the credits you have against the circulating wealth of the nation. When you take money out of your pocket and exchange it for some commodity, you automatically debit your own account and credit the merchant's account.

Money, then, is a *unit of account* used in trade. To explain what this means, think of the yard as the unit of account for lengths or the ounce as the unit of account for weights; they are both arbitrary quantities by which we may measure lengths and weights. In the same way, the dollar (or the pound, the yen, the euro, etc.) is just the arbitrary number chosen so that we may weigh and measure the economy. We measure the total output of the economy (the Gross Domestic Product or GDP) in terms of this measure, and our own claims against this output in terms of our own income measured in dollars. Hence, like the yard or the ounce, the dollar or the euro has no natural measure; it is an arbitrarily chosen unit.

The idea of money as a unit of account, however, really understates its power to effect change and to bring new goods to market. Think about a situation where there are unused lands, unemployed men, idle tools, sufficient raw materials, and consumers waiting for the goods they could produce. These unemployed assets we may think of as *real savings,* things held out of production but which could be put to use. But it is unlikely that they will be put to use unless there are some *monetary savings.* That is, without the bits of paper or the electronic blips, the men will remain unemployed, the tools unused, the land idle, and the market unsatisfied. Money then contains the power to command these resources and to call new products into being, and those who control money, can control everything else. This power can come from two sources: money can be saved or money can be created. A person who saves will gain some power over real goods and services, but it will be a small power in relation to a person who can simply create money. Money does need to be created; it is not a natural commodity. And the question of who has this power of money creation is a crucial one in understanding any economy. More of this question in a moment.

Inflation and Deflation

There is one essential difference between money and the other units of account. We do not expect the length of the yard or the weight of the ounce to change. But the value of money does change, and on a daily, indeed, moment-to-moment basis. This is because the economy, unlike the things measured by ounces or yards, changes from moment to moment. Our dollar represents our claims against the goods and services produced, but the amount of these goods and services, as well as the number of claims against them, are constantly changing. What the unit of account measures, in the case of money, is the *ratio* between things claimed and the number of claims (dollars), both of which are constantly changing.

If the supply of money increases faster than the goods and services for sale, then inflation is the result; if it increases more slowly than the goods for sale, deflation is the result. Inflation simply means that prices are rising, while deflation means that they are falling. Inflation penalizes savers (whose savings can purchase less) and helps borrowers (who pay back their loans in dollars worth less than the ones they borrowed); deflation does the reverse. Inflation tends to benefit the young (who often must contract large debts to finance an education or establish a home and family). At the same time, inflation can reduce the value of savings. Deflation tends to be very hard on the young, since it increases the value of their debts but lowers the value of their labor.

In any case, the supply of money should expand (or contract) no faster than the increase (or decrease) in the supply of circulating goods and services. Note that the supply of money is composed of two factors. One is simply the amount of money available to spend. The other factor is the speed at which it is spent, called the *efficiency* or the *velocity* of money. So for example, if in a given economy there are one million units of money (dollars, shekels, euros, etc.) and in a year's time each unit changes hands ten times, then there are ten million units in purchasing power. But if each unit changes hands twenty times, then there are twenty million units in purchasing power for that year. The velocity of money is largely a function of the psychology of consumers and investors. In good times, they tend to spend money quickly, and in bad times they are reluctant to spend at all.

In order to prevent rapid changes in the value of the money, that is, inflation or deflation, it is necessary to keep the growth of the money supply roughly in line with the growth of goods and services for sale. This is where things begin to get sticky. Just how does one limit the money supply to the actual value of the actually circulating goods? When we actually examine the things we call "money," what we see are scraps of paper and bits of base metals. The scraps of paper are called (in England and elsewhere) "banknotes." We don't call them that in the United States, but if you look at the top of each dollar, you will see the words "Federal Reserve Note." The Federal Reserve is the national bank, so these too are banknotes. Why should banknotes be "money," how are they supplied to the market, and who manages the supply, if management is needed? To answer these questions, we need to understand how money is created in our system.

Money and Fractional Reserve Banking

Henry Ford found the system of money creation so appalling that he said if people understood how it worked, there would be a revolution before breakfast. What is the fact that Ford found so repugnant? It is simply this: before you sign the mortgage to buy your home, the note to buy your car, or the credit slip at McDonald's to buy a hamburger, the money to buy the home, the car, or the burger does not exist; it comes into being in the very act of borrowing it. In other words, the banks create money.[3]

How does this happen? First, let us look at the history of modern money. In that glorious age before bankers, money tended to be not bits of paper, but gold and silver coins. But gold and silver are difficult to store securely and dangerous to carry, so people often deposited their coins with goldsmiths who had safes in which to store the metals. The goldsmith would give the depositor a "note" of how much he had on deposit. If the goldsmith was of good reputation in the area, these notes could circulate as money, since buyers and sellers knew that they could get their gold from the smith if they really needed it, and they felt better with the paper than with the gold. The goldsmiths noticed, however, that they didn't actually need to hold all the gold, because it was unlikely that everybody would ask for their gold back at the same time. They only needed a small fraction of what they held, and could lend out the rest at interest. Indeed, they could lend it all, and lend it several times. So the goldsmith might give the depositor a note for his one thousand gold ducats, and also lend the same one thousand ducats to someone else in the form of notes. In fact, he may have lent the same ducats many times over, in the form of notes. So long as they all didn't come looking for their gold at the same time, the goldsmith could become very wealthy very easily, and all with somebody else's money. Through trial and error, the goldsmiths discovered that they could lend the same coin out about ten times without too much trouble. This induced many of the smiths to abandon the forge completely and become full-time bankers.

It may seem like a very dangerous procedure to lend out the same ducat ten times, but actually, it could be very sound. If the borrowed money was used for productive purposes, if it was used to build a factory or a road or a ship, then the supply of goods and the supply of money increased at about the same rate. But if the money was used merely to finance consumption, then there was an expansion in the supply of money with no corresponding direct contribution to the expansion of production. In this case (called "usury") the money supply grew faster than the supply of goods and inflation was the result. But whether for usury or for production, the banks were expanding the supply of money faster than the supply of gold on deposit. Hence "money" became not the gold on deposit that the notes were supposed to represent, but the notes themselves, mere scraps of paper.

This discussion may seem quaint and out-of-date, but in fact the exact same thing happens today. Banks create money through *fractional reserve banking,* which is a long phrase for the same process. You deposit $100,000 with the bank. The bank keeps a portion on reserve and lends the rest. If the reserve requirement is 10 percent, the bank keeps $10,000 in its vaults as a reserve, and lends out $90,000. But the bank doesn't actually give the borrower the $90,000 he has borrowed; rather, it creates a *credit* of $90,000 against which the borrower may write checks. So now there is an additional $90,000 on deposit, of which the bank reserves $9,000 and lends out $81,000. The original $100,000 deposit is quickly multiplied into loans of $900,000, for a total of $1 million on deposit.[4]

One might raise the objection here that the borrowers do indeed take their money out of the bank. But in truth they don't, or rather, they don't take it out of the banking system. What they generally do is write checks against these new deposits, which are then presented to other banks, to become deposits at that bank. But these other banks also trade checks with the first bank, creating new deposits. At the end of each day, when the banks total up their total checks paid against the total checks received for the day, they might have an excess or a deficit in their required reserves. They then lend or borrow money overnight from each other or from the Federal Reserve Bank to keep their reserve accounts in order.

Most people think that money is created by the government. The government does indeed have the power to do so, but exercises that power only in the case of the coinage and in some other rare cases. Money creation is a monopoly of the private banking system. This leads to any number of problems, but the most immediate is that the banks have no "natural" way of matching the growth of the money supply to the actual growth (or shrinkage) in real goods and services available. Indeed, it is in the banks' best interest to create as much money as they can, regardless of what is happening in the rest of the economy. What actually happens is that in good times, the banks create too much money, thereby fueling booms and inflation, and in bad times, they make very few loans, leading to deflation and deepening recessions. In order to maintain some control over the money supply, all governments which have a fractional reserve banking system (which today are all governments) also have a *central bank* to try to influence the supply of money. In the United States, that bank is called the Federal Reserve Bank.

The Federal Reserve Bank

The Federal Reserve Bank is sometimes called "The Creature from Jekyll Island" because the plans for its formation were drawn up in great secrecy in 1910 by the prominent bankers at an isolated retreat in Georgia called Jekyll Island.[5] The bankers were impelled to action by the instability of the gold-based banking system. Since gold is a limited commodity, its supply could not expand as quickly as could economic activity. This led to a long period of chronic deflation, which destroyed both farmer and small merchant. Wheat sold for $2.06 per bushel in 1866, but only got 80 cents in the 1880s and as low as 35 cents in the 1890s.[6] While the prices the farmers received fell, however, the value of their debts rose. Moreover, since money was usually in short supply, interest rates were ruinous, and year after year the farmers found that their labor produced fewer returns. The original idea for a national bank came from the populist movement of the nineteenth century, as a way of increasing the money supply. The populists never got very far with their idea, which would have the government issue money directly, apart from the gold standard. But in the early twentieth century, the New York banks revived the idea, except that it would not be the government, but the banks that issued the new money under a fractional reserve system.

The bankers wanted a central bank with legal powers but completely independent of the federal government. What actually resulted from the negotiations with President Wilson and Congress was a hybrid institution. The Federal Reserve is not actually a part of the federal government, despite its name. Rather, it is a private institution, but with legal authority and is only indirectly controlled by the public power. The Federal Reserve is a system of twelve regional banks which are owned by all the federally chartered banks in that region. To get a federal bank charter, the bank must buy shares in the Federal Reserve Bank for their region. Each bank elects its own board of directors. But the seven members of the Board of Governors for the whole system are appointed by the president of the United States for fourteen-year terms, and the chairman and vice chairman of the board are appointed by the president from among the members of the board to four year terms.[7] Monetary policy for the United States is set by the Federal Open Market Committee (FOMC), which consists of the seven members of the board, plus five of the regional bank presidents, one of whom is always the president of the New York Federal Reserve Bank (which owns 53 percent of the Federal Reserve System) and the other four positions are rotated among the other bank presidents.

While the "The Fed" (as it is called) has many supervisory functions over the banking system, its most public function is to influence the money supply. For this task, the FOMC has three major tools: the "discount rate" (the interest rate banks are charged for borrowing money from the Fed); "open market operations" (directly injecting or withdrawing money into the economy by buying or selling government bonds to or from the banks); and changing the amount of reserves that banks are required to hold. In extreme cases (such as what is occurring today), the bank can actually "print" money by creating credits on its books with which to buy bonds from the Treasury Department. Taken together, these measures provide a crude form of influencing the money supply. But despite the uncertainty of central bank controls, every country that has a fractional reserve system also has a central bank, because this is the only way to inject any rationality into the monopoly money-creation system. But the major function of the bank is the one that is nowhere explicitly stated: it is to legitimate the near-monopoly that the banks have over the creation of money.

Money as Debt

The fractional reserve system means that virtually all money is created as a debt, which means that all money carries an interest rate to the banks. But this creates a problem, since each new loan creates the principle, but not the interest. The interest payments must come from further loans, and their interest payments presume even more loans. This creates the "impossible contract." For example, if I borrow $1,000 for a year at 10 percent simple interest, I must pay back $1,100. The $1,000 was injected into the economy by the first loan, but the $100 interest payment was not. Somebody else had to borrow the $100, but that requires a $110 payment, which means that someone else had to borrow $10. In other words, loans must constantly be supplied to the economy for the purpose of paying off the interest on old loans. Eventually, the system gets over-extended and a credit crisis is the result. Such crises are built into the DNA of a debt money situation. It usually happens, however, that the people who most suffer from such a credit recession are not the same group as those who profited from the money expansion. In other words, the rewards are privatized, but the risks are socialized: the winners get to keep their winnings, but the public is required to cover the losses.

The ability of bankers to create money out of thin air also provides for a "perverse incentive," that is, an incentive that encourages people to engage in risky or harmful behaviors. The banks make their profit from the interest on money they create, so the more loans they can make, the more profit. But there may not always be sufficient productive opportunities to absorb the amount of money they are willing to lend. Hence, the banks are always tempted to lend for purely speculative purposes, such as stock market or currency speculation, activities which add no real goods and services to the economy, yet can be profitable, at least for awhile. This increases the supply of money relative to the real goods available, and hence leads to inflation.

The most famous example of this was the German hyper-inflation of 1922–23. The German mark went from a value of 4.2 to the dollar to 2.5 *trillion* to the dollar.[8] While the story is a rather complex one, with many twists and turns, it originates with Germany's defeat in World War I. The allies insisted that the Reichsbank, roughly the German central bank, be privatized. Only a privatized bank, it was believed, could establish a sound currency. But events proved otherwise. All government controls were removed from the Reichsbank in May, 1922, and the problems began almost immediately. Speculators began *short-selling* German money financed by loans they obtained from the Reichsbank itself. "Short-selling" is a process of selling some financial instrument, stocks, bonds, currencies, and the like, which the seller does not happen to own. Since there is a period of several days between the sale and requirement to actually deliver the instrument, the seller hopes to drive down its value and make a profit. Since short-sellers are selling what they don't actually own, they make it appear that the supply of the given financial instrument is larger than it really is. If they do it in sufficiently large volumes, they drive up the apparent supply and hence lower the price. Short-selling can therefore be a self-fulfilling prophecy. But the short-sellers need to borrow large sums to finance this game, and the Reichsbank could not resist the temptation to lend them this money, even though it meant the destruction of the German currency; it is an example of the power of perverse incentives.

While this story may seem remote, it is largely what happened during the current crisis, as banks lent huge sums to hedge funds and other financial speculators. The American banks added a twist of their own. Normally, a loan is a liability on the books of the bank, but the banks turned the loans into cash by "securitizing" them, that is, by converting them into bonds and selling them. This is the famous "alphabet soup" of financial instruments with which we have all become too familiar, such as CDOs (Collateralized Debt Obligations) and MBSs (Mortgage Backed Securities), among other clever instruments. By selling these instruments, the banks converted liabilities into cash, and then were able to use the cash to make yet more loans. Indeed, they lent huge sums to hedge funds to buy these instruments, in much the same way that the Reichsbank lent the money to short the mark. But when the underlying loans failed, the hedge funds collapsed and the loans couldn't be repaid; the banks failed and demanded that the government bail them out, yet another demonstration of the perverse incentives involved with private money creation.

Debt money has another effect: the government must borrow its money just like everybody else, and hence it must pay interest like everybody else. These interest charges are now about half a trillion dollars and constitute the largest single government expenditure except for the defense budget. In order to pay the interest, the government has three options: cut back on services, raise taxes, or borrow more money. The first two choices are often very difficult politically and may have genuinely negative social and economic consequences. This leaves only the third option, which of course just makes the problem worse. Further, borrowing just passes the problem on to the next generation, which is morally questionable, to say the least. Is there any way out of this conundrum? Must we borrow to the point of collapse, and then start over again?

Government-Created Money

Governments can create money. They can "print" the money, creating it out of thin air as credits, just as the banks do. Many people fear this, labeling it "fiat" money. And while this is true, it is only trivially true: *all* money is fiat money, even gold coins. All money is man-made (fiat), and it makes as much sense to worry about fiat money as it does to worry about fiat homes or iPods. There is a legitimate concern about money, government-created or otherwise, and that involves controlling the supply, as we have seen. But when the government creates its own money, the amount of money created is well known and the responsibility for inflation or deflation is well-established.

If the government prints money for its capital improvements, the public is not saddled with interest payments to a group of private citizens who happen to control the money supply. This need not be inflationary *if* the new money is used solely for the purposes of expanding the public infrastructure, since this expands the productive capacity of the nation. This might be a small and temporary amount of inflation, since money is not wealth, but merely a claim on circulating wealth. You do not build roads and bridges out of money; you build them out of steel and concrete. Issuing new money redirects some of the concrete and steel away from the private sector and into the public sector. By increasing the demand for these commodities, it is likely also to increase the price. Assuming that the infrastructure helps to create new wealth, however, the increase in the supply of goods is likely to quickly catch up with the supply of new money, mitigating any inflationary effects. Recall the example where there are unused land, labor, and tools in the economy ("real" savings) but no money with which to bring them together. As long as there are such unused resources, money can be produced to actuate the productive power of such resources without undue risk of inflation. Furthermore, such spending of new money can be used as a method to invigorate a faltering economy. When the economy is weak, the government can simply invest new money in worthwhile projects, and do so without either borrowing money or increasing taxes.

Is Gold Money?

There are those who believe that a return to the gold standard and the abolition of paper money would solve all of these problems; they believe that this would make money less of a fictitious commodity and more of a real one, since gold has an "intrinsic" value, apart from any government or bank manipulation. Further, they argue that a gold currency would remove the power to create new money from the banks or anybody else, thereby stabilizing the money supply. Finally, the "gold bugs" argue that history is on their side. For most of history, and in most advanced cultures, money was usually stamped out in gold coins.

These arguments are easy to counter. Gold's "intrinsic" value is largely artistic, since gold has little use outside of the decorative arts. In fact, one reason for using gold as money is that it didn't have very many other uses, and hence would not conflict with any productive use of the metal. Moreover, when money was gold, governments set its value, not the market. In the case of gold coins, the nominal value of gold was whatever number the prince stamped on the coin. A coin that said "10" was worth ten (ducats, lire, dollars, whatever), and this number was the official price for gold of that weight. In the era of paper money, the gold-paper exchange rate was always set by the government; there was no market in gold, and certainly no "commodity" money in gold. When gold was money, it was not a commodity, and when it was a commodity (as it is today) it was not money.

The gold bugs are right that a gold currency would fix the supply of money, but this sounds more like an argument against it. A dynamic economy needs a dynamic money supply; nothing will kill an expansion more quickly that a limited supply of currency.

Finally, the historical argument is not as strong as it might seem at first glance. Many prosperous cultures did not use gold, or did not use it exclusively. China, for example, relied on bronze. Indeed, the historical argument would seem to work against a gold standard. In the first place, the argument ignores what the goldsmiths, and later the bankers, actually did. They still used paper money with only paper-thin reserves of gold. Further, a strict adherence to the gold standard was part of the economic orthodoxy of the nineteenth and early twentieth centuries. It was a disaster, destabilizing economies all over the globe. In America, prices fluctuated wildly, with inflation whenever a new gold strike was discovered and deflation the rest of the time. The supply of money was related not to the needs of the economy, but to the chance of discovering new sources of gold. All social classes came to reject it, and none more than the capitalist classes, whose businesses simply could not tolerate the wild fluctuations that resulted from a dogmatically applied gold standard. The plain fact is that no nation is likely to be able to expand its supply of gold as fast as it can expand its productive capacity. The gold standard then becomes a throttle on the expansion of the economy. As nice as the "real money" of gold sounds, there really is no way to make a fictitious commodity a real one. We can really go no further than Aristotle did 2,500 years ago, when he declared that money is not a commodity, but exists only by law or custom. Money, then, is not an intrinsic power of some commodity, it is a necessary power of the community. As such, it will either be the democratic power of the whole community, or an oligarchic power of a few members of the community.

Money and Community

But if money is not backed by gold, then what does back it? The answer is simple: anything you can buy with money. This tells us who should have the power to create money: anyone who produces goods and services for which the money can be exchanged. In one sense, every producer does have this power, for when a merchant extends credit to his clients, he creates money to that extent, money backed by the goods he offers for sale. Airlines create money in the form of airline mileage credits, which are backed by the seats they offer for sale.

The problem with airline miles is that the airline itself has absolute control over the value of the money; they control its value by varying the number of seats for which they will redeem the coupons. Often, one finds few seats available at the nominal value, and must pay a higher rate to get the flight that is actually useful. Since the value is controlled to meet the needs of the issuer, most people are unwilling to use things like airline miles as a general currency, however attractive they may find it as a supplemental currency. Most businesses do not want the trouble or risk of issuing their own money, and they prefer that the privilege be deferred to some public power. But it is important that they have the right. Indeed, the right of money creation is a right of any goods-producing community. Note that I said "community" rather than "government." The government is a community, and hence has the rights of a community, but it does not have these rights exclusively, or it displaces all other communities. Federal governments take to themselves a monopoly right of money creation (which monopoly they then delegate to the banks) but it is not necessary for them to do so. Since the government can declare its own currency the only acceptable one for the payment of taxes, and since we all pay taxes, their currency will always have a preeminence.

Communities other than the federal government should have the power to issue money, and there is often good reason for them to do so. Local currencies stay within the community and activate local resources. This theory was given a test in the town of Wörgl, Austria, in 1933. In the depths of the Great Depression, economic activity had pretty much come to a stop. The town then issued its own currency, and things immediately revived.[9] Indeed, the new money was spent so quickly and revived economic activity so completely that the town authorities first thought that the money was being counterfeited. But it wasn't; it was being spent, and spent rapidly. The experiment spread to surrounding towns and attracted national and international interest. The Austrian government, however, outlawed the new currency as a threat to the national currency. It wasn't, of course, since the new money was redeemable in Austrian schillings, if anyone needed to do so. But it was a threat to the bankers' monopoly over money.

The Wörgl experience does reveal a truth about recessions: they are largely monetary phenomena. There were no fewer resources in Wörgl before the depression than during it; they had roughly the same amounts of land, labor, and tools. But as money had stopped circulating, these things could not be brought together to produce goods and services. The new money circulated very quickly and so revived the economy.

So who should have the authority to issue money? Anybody or any community that has a stock of goods and services for which the money may be redeemed. Obviously there need to be legal controls. But the greatest legal control is simply the removal of "limited liability." Any issuer of money must put his own personal fortune at the hazard. If the directors of the banks had their own money at risk, they would be very conservative indeed in how they issued money and to whom they lent it.

8

The Fictitious Commodities: Labor

Is All Unemployment Voluntary?

One of the more curious conclusions of neoclassical and Austrian economics is that all unemployment is voluntary. Although this seems startling, it is a logical and necessary conclusion from their premises. *If* labor is a commodity like any other, and *if* all commodities have a market-clearing price (a price that would increase demand enough to clear all the goods offered for sale) then labor also must have a market-clearing price. Hence, if there is unemployment, it can only mean that workers are demanding more than the market price, and hence their unemployment must be considered voluntary. If they would only lower their wage demands, everyone who wanted a job would have one, albeit at a wage less than they would like. Therefore chronic unemployment can only be the result of workers who demand too much and employers who cave in to their demands. As the prominent economics lecturer Paul Heyne put it:

[T]he quantity of labor supplied [is] chronically greater than the quantity demanded, principally because many employers have strong incentives to offer wage rates higher than the rates that would clear the market.[1]

In Heyne's world, unemployment is caused "principally" by greedy workers and compliant employers.

If Heyne and his fellow economists are correct, if labor really is a commodity like any other, then we would expect to see high employment rates associated with low wages, and low employment with high wages. We should see low-wage economies having both the lowest unemployment rates and the highest labor participation rates (that is, a higher percentage of adults in the workforce). But what we actually see is precisely the opposite. Both employment and participation rates are usually higher in high-wage economies, while unemployment seems to rise as wages fall. The demand for labor seems to vary *with* its price, not inversely to it. Causation runs *not* from wages to employment, but from employment to wages. Lowering wages does not increase employment; only the prospect of selling more goods induces employers to take on more hands. And in general, more goods are sold when more people have jobs—the better the jobs, the better the prospect of increased sales.

There are, of course, limits. Wages cannot be raised to any arbitrary amount, even for the purpose of improving the economy. There are three natural limits on wages:

- Wages cannot exceed the income of the firm; a firm cannot pay out more in wages than it receives in income, at least not for any appreciable length of time.
- Wages cannot displace the legitimate returns to capital, or capital will simply withdraw from the market. Capital, after all, is simply prior-period labor, and deserves a return no less than current-period (actual) labor. Their respective rights are not opposed to each other, but spring from the same source.

- Wages cannot far exceed the *capital substitution rate,* which simply means that at some point it is cheaper to use more machines and fewer workers.

The first two limits embody an aspect of equity. In the first case, it would be iniquitous to simply bankrupt the firm. In the second, there needs to be equity between capital and labor, or the economy cannot reach equilibrium, or at least not by economic means. This equity is easier to reach if we only keep in mind that capital is merely labor in a different form.

Wages and the Supply of Labor

If labor is not supplied to the market according to the "commodity" supply and demand curves, then how is it supplied? The amount of work each person is willing to supply is an individual decision. The following four charts depict the supply curves for four different kinds of workers:[2]

The first chart is for a surfer whose goal in life is to indulge his passion for surfing. He lives in a crowded apartment near the beach

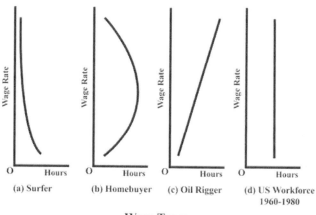

Wage Types

with a few surfing buddies. By pooling their resources, they can give the market one or two days' casual labor a week and spend the rest of their time surfing. As wages rise, he actually gives less labor, not more; his needs can be met with less work, which allows him to devote more time to his "real work" of perfecting his surfing technique. This chart is labeled "surfer," but it could just as easily be labeled "artist," "poet," or anybody who has a passion for something that exceeds his or her desire for material comforts.

The second chart represents a worker intent on buying a home. As wages rise, this becomes more of a possibility, and he is willing to give more hours up until the point that he has enough for the down payment. After that, an increase in wages actually produces less work, and he devotes more time to his family and their new home.

The third chart represents a worker on a remote oil platform working to gather as much money as possible in the shortest amount of time, perhaps to buy a house, start a business, or just to take a year or two off. Increasing wages will call forth more effort.

The fourth chart represents the mass of citizens who give their forty hours of work a week regardless of what the wage rates are. If they want more income, they look to promotions, wage increases, or better jobs rather than more hours.

This provides a rather chaotic view of the supply of work. Is there anyway to unite these four charts under a common supply curve? I believe there is. Take our supply chart and draw on it four lines, labeled "subsistence," "comfort," "security," and "wealth." These lines represent the wage at which each of these things is attainable. Of course, the definition of each of these lines will vary from person to person. For our surfer friend, the "subsistence" and "wealth" lines are identical, because he attains wealth when he gets enough to allow him to surf. For the home buyer, wealth is achieved with the new home, after which the supply curve bends back on itself. For the rigger, wealth is achieved, if it is achieved, only after he earns enough to meet his goal. The mass of workers in an advanced and relatively stable economy work in the zone between security and wealth; hence, increasing wages do not call forth much of an increase in the hours of work, and what increases it does pro-

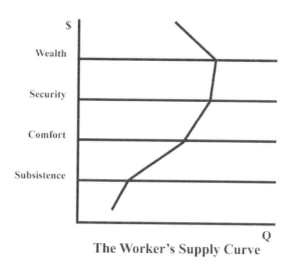

The Worker's Supply Curve

duce are balanced by losses from those who have passed the wealth line. Each of our workers is working along a different segment of the curve. Although the definitions of each line vary, there is nevertheless within any society a tacit, if imprecise, recognition of where these levels lie.

A few observations about this unified curve: We may note that wages below subsistence do not call forth much work, and even less loyalty or quality. Secondly, the curve bends backward at the wealth line. *All* supply and demand curves are backward bending. At some point, an increase in price will *not* produce an increase in supply; at another point, a decline in price will *not* call forth an increase in demand. This is called the law of diminishing returns, and it is part of every economic curve, although one almost never sees it drawn in supply and demand curves.

Another implication of this chart is that people do not define themselves exclusively in terms of paid work. At some point (barring the outright pathological), they have enough, and devote their time to other things, usually unpaid work like families, hobbies, and volunteer work. We happen to live in a consumerist society, and we can define consumerism as the attempt to manipulate public perceptions, to move the security and wealth lines "northwards" so that people will always feel insecure and poor, and hence will devote more of their time to paid work and more of their money to consumer products. This is not, however, a "natural" condition for humans. It takes a tremendous amount of miseducation, usually in the form of advertising and social manipulation, to convince people that their happiness lies exclusively in "things" rather than persons. Aside from being a tremendous drag on the economy, because the billions of dollars devoted to advertising compete with funds for productive uses, this view also distorts our view of work.

Finally, we can note that from the standpoint of the employer, the greatest gains come where wages are kept at the subsistence line. It is at this point that the smallest gains in wages produce the greatest gains in work. Employers tend to believe, if only implicitly, that it is in their best interest to keep wages in between the subsistence and comfort lines, leaving the worker with less security and hence greater dependence on the employer. This is, of course, a misperception, because, as G. K. Chesterton points out, "in cutting down what his servant demands," the employer is also cutting down "what his customer can spend."[3] More simply, laborer and consumer are the same person. By keeping wages down balance is lost, and the gains to the employer are matched by losses to the overall economy.

Work and the Worker

The economist's basic assumption about commodified labor is that people are averse to work; work represents a "disutility," something to be avoided. As Jeremy Bentham put it, "Aversion is the emotion—the only emotion—which *labour,* taken by itself, is qualified to produce . . . *love of labour* is a contradiction in terms."[4] This aversion must be overcome either with the threat of starvation or, when that is not possible, with the promise of high rewards. The irony of this statement is that Bentham labored long and hard to write it, and did so despite the fact that no one was paying him for it. The truth is that people love to work. A man will come home from a hard day's labor and immediately go out to his workshop or into his garden. Or if he is truly weird, he will sit down and write books on political economy. But people love to accomplish things; they love to contribute; they love to demonstrate their skills and their mastery over some productive technique. Most of us find pure idleness difficult and disheartening, and we seek work even if no one will pay us for it. It is only since the invention of the television that people could be diverted enough from the boredom of idleness to engage in it for very long.

Man is not averse to work in itself, but rather work performed under degrading or oppressive conditions, work that is boring and repetitive, work that calls for no exercise of the mind, work that is not recognized for the contribution it makes, or where the worker himself is valued as no more than a cog in a machine. Managers schooled in modern economics will perceive these aversions to certain forms of work as an aversion to work itself, and they will apply the wrong organizational and managerial techniques to overcome an "aversion" that does not, in fact, exist.

Are Mothers Useless?

In chapter 4, we introduced John Mueller's economic stork theory (EST), which demonstrated that economists have no way to account for the arrival of workers in the economy. Even as they "commodify" the worker, economists have no way to account for the "production" of this "commodity"; the worker just mysteriously "appears" in the economy. Economists are willing to talk about the production of other "commodities," such as pigs or pig iron. They know that the price of these commodities must cover the cost of production, maintenance, and depreciation, or the commodity will simply disappear from the market. When it comes to labor, however, they are reluctant to concede that this too is "produced" and has production, maintenance, and depreciation costs. In other words, they commodify labor, and then refuse to speak of it as they would any other commodity. Hence, even under its own terms, the neoclassical theory is incomplete; it cannot account for this rather basic "commodity" per se, but must accept its creation out of thin air.

Mueller's economic stork theory has a rather curious corollary. Under the EST, the only useful work done in the economy is work done for wages or other economic rewards, and hence there are only two kinds of human activity, work and leisure.[5] Thus, there are only two kinds of individuals in this theory, what I call *Partially Useful Individuals* (PUIs) and *Totally Useless Individuals* (TUIs). The PUIs are partially useful because they spend some of their time at "work" producing things in the exchange economy. The TUIs, however, don't "work" at all. Rather, some of the TUIs, otherwise known as "mothers," spend their time in such leisure activities as taking care of the household pets; some of these pets are called "cats" or "dogs," and others are called "children," another form of TUIs.

Since the standard of living in the EST is the result of a positive capital-to-labor ratio, increasing the number of PUIs does not increase the standard of living unless the amount of capital is increased by at least an equal amount. In other words, you can increase the standard of living by decreasing the number of people, or at least slowing the growth of the population. Therefore the crucial element in growth is capital, and people stunt that growth. The policy implications are that capital should not be taxed, only people, in the form of labor or consumption taxes. This will help to discourage the formation of new PUI/TUIs, while raising the capital-to-labor ratio.

Use and Exchange

Mueller points out that the EST's most glaring error is its failure to recognize that the family is the basic economic unit. Within the family, the choice is not so much between work and leisure as it is between *production for exchange* and *production for use.* Of course, economic theory simply has no way to account for production for use, even though it is actually the whole point of production for exchange; we work to provide money to buy meat and potatoes which we then use to produce dinner. Production for use does not show up in the GDP, but in fact the GDP presupposes such production. Indeed, production for use is the largest single segment of the economy, even though it appears in no economic table or government report. What the TUIs, known as mothers, do is crucial not just to the continuation of the economic system, but to the continuation of civilization itself. Moreover, the social shifts of the last fifty years have moved us away from production for use to production for exchange. One may debate as long as one likes the soundness of this move into the workplace in terms of, say, women's liberation, however, as the feminists point out (quite rightly), if mothers were paid for everything they do, they would earn a hefty salary indeed. But the attempt to monetize the work of mothers, to convert it from production for use to production for exchange, is futile and leads to endless debates that have no possible resolution. There simply isn't enough money to replace what mothers do everyday. The transfer of work from use to exchange does indeed show up as an "increase" in the GDP, but not as an increase in any actual output of goods and services, and likely involves an actual *decrease* in such services and their quality. Do day care centers really provide the same level of care as does a family? Do fast-food stands really substitute for family meals?

Moreover, the policy implications are obvious. Differential rates of taxation between capital and consumption (or labor) misallocate resources and send the wrong signals. If you have the good fortune to be a robot, your income would be calculated by deducting the costs of your production, maintenance, and depreciation from your net receipts. But since you are merely a human, these expenses are treated with contempt by the taxing authorities and by the economic theories on which they rest. Children become a "consumer item" rather than an economic resource, and hence are not supported with the same policy care that is devoted to capital.

In sum, the attempt to commodify labor posits a relationship between wages and work that does not, in fact, exist; there is no equilibrium point determined exclusively by supply and demand when it comes to labor. Hence, wages are not set by this curve; we will discuss in a later chapter how wages are really set. Moreover, commodified labor distorts human relations that do exist and upon which the entire economic structure rests. We end up devaluing both the worker and his or her family, and advancing policies which degrade both in favor of capital. A society that degrades the family degrades its own future. And if it does not reverse its course, it will have no future.

9

The Fictitious Commodities:
Land

What Ever Happened to Land?

I have in hand the popular economics textbook, *The Economic Way of Thinking*.[1] Looking at the index, I find no entry for land. Having read the book, I happen to know that there are scattered references to land, but not enough to warrant an index entry. Searching for "property" yields only marginally better results. It does have an index entry referring to scattered and fragmentary mentions, but there is no sustained treatment of the topic, no inquiry as to what it is, where it comes from, what rights it ought to have—and ought *not* to have—and what place it plays in the political economy. What is odd about this is that land had been a staple of economic science from the days of Aristotle up through the early part of the twentieth century, when the topic abruptly disappeared. Land suddenly became just another species of capital, and one that required no special treatment or explanation.

Land, however, is not at all like any other bit of capital. Capital is something made by human hands and is consumed in the process of production. Land is neither made by humans nor consumed in production.

Further, capital can, in theory, be infinitely expanded; we can always make new tools. But land is fixed in its supply. If you wish to have land in some place, say Manhattan, you must find someone with existing rights to land and either purchase or lease those rights. Another difference is that there is no substitute for land. Capital and labor may be substituted for one another, and different kinds of commodities may be used in place of each other. For example, if the price of steel is too high, we may decide to make some things from plastic instead; if the price of beef is too high, we may decide to eat chicken instead. But we cannot substitute anything for land. Land is required for all production, and permits no substitutions. Even in the infinite space of cyberspace, we still need a place to house the servers, the towers, the lines, and so forth.

Land, still further, has another strange characteristic: it increases in value whether or not it is used, while the returns from capital and labor can only come from their use. In fact, quite often the best returns come from withholding land from use, that is, from speculation. It is precisely this characteristic of the land that could not be reconciled with neoclassical economics. The neoclassicals had a method of allocating rewards between capital and labor based on their beliefs about the contribution each made to production. But that theory simply could not be reconciled with land. Hence, in order to maintain the theory, it was necessary to get rid of land as a separate category, and to treat it—when it was treated at all—as another form of capital. In a later chapter, we will examine why the theory does not apply either to wages or profits, but for now, we need to see why it does not—and cannot—apply to land.

The Supply and Demand for Land

One test we have been using for a "fictitious commodity" is whether or not we can draw a "normal" supply and demand diagram for that commodity. When we look at the chart for land, we immediately notice that this is very different from a normal commodity supply and demand

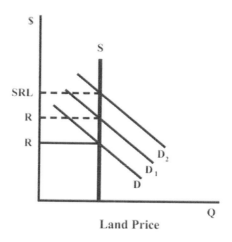

Land Price

chart. The first difference is that the supply curve is simply a vertical line, which represents the fact that the supply of land is fixed and does not vary with the price. The second difference is that instead of one demand curve, we have three. Since there is a fixed supply of land, you can't move *along* the demand curve; each increase in demand means shifting the whole curve "northward" to establish a new demand curve. At any given moment, the curve D represents the demand for land in a given area. At the point it crosses the supply curve, we draw a horizontal line to the left and read the general level of rents and prices for land. When the demand for land increases (or falls), we don't move to a new point on the demand curve but establish a new curve (D_1) above or below the old demand line D and read a new rent level at R_1. So we already have a big difference between the land supply and demand chart and that of a "normal" commodity. However, there is one more line on this chart that we will not find on the others. It is labeled "D_2"

and its corresponding rent line is labeled "SRL" for Speculative Rent Line. I will have more to say about this line, but first there are some questions that we must answer about land:

- How is land priced?
- What is the relationship between rent and wages?
- What causes changes in the demand for land?

We also need to be clear about the subject. When we buy or rent a home or a building, the price or rent we pay is normally one amount. However, that one amount is actually in two parts. One part is for the building itself. Monies paid for a building are simply a return to capital and are governed by the same laws of supply and demand that cover any real commodity. The other part of the payment is for the land underneath the building, usually called the *ground rent*. It is only the ground rent that concerns us here, which we may define as the price of the property exclusive of any on-site improvements. Our first question, then, is, "How is this ground rent determined?"

The Law of (Ground) Rents

The law of rents operates in a private property economy. It was first articulated by David Ricardo at the beginning of the nineteenth century and became a staple of economic theory. There are many long tomes and learned treatises written on this law, but it is actually based on an intuitively obvious idea, even though it leads to a counterintuitive result. The intuitive idea is that between two parcels of land with different productivities, the parcel with the higher productivity will command a higher rent. In other words, if you can grow more corn, or otherwise do more business, on plot A than you can on plot B, then the landlord will charge more for A than for B. How much more? This is the surprising part. The difference in rent will tend to equal the difference in productivity. That is, if plot A produces one hundred fifty bushels of corn, and plot B only one hundred bushels, then plot A will rent for fifty bushels more than plot B. This means that all increases in productivity tend to go to the landlord, and the returns to the renters from all parcels of land in a given market tend to be equalized. Can this be true?

Take a set of building plans and build the identical building in downtown New York, downtown Dallas, downtown Laredo, and out in the middle of the desert. Clearly, they will garner different rents. The building in the desert will likely get no rent at all, while the one in New York will get a very high rent, with Dallas and Laredo in between. The difference in the rents of these buildings cannot be attributed to anything intrinsic to the buildings themselves, since they are identical. The only possible explanation of the difference is in the ground rent. So far, none of this is contentious, and few would disagree.

The law of rents rests on three assumptions:

- Land is necessary for production.
- Land has varying productivities.
- Demand is rational, informed, mobile, and driven by considerations of financial value.[2]

The first two assumptions appear to be self-evident. The third is the assumption of the perfect market, and to the extent that it is true, the law of rents will be true. Of course, markets are never perfect, so the law of rents will never operate perfectly; nevertheless, there will always be a strong tendency for rent to absorb all increases in productivity.

Just how much can rent absorb? Look at the following chart.

On the horizontal axis, all parcels of land are ordered by their productivity given by the diagonal line at the top, which indicates the total product of any particular site. A, B, C, and M are parcels of land. M is the least productive site that is capable of providing a subsistence wage. It can collect no rent and no parcel less productive will be worked. This

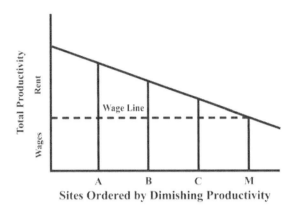

Sites Ordered by Dimishing Productivity

is called the "Margin of Production." From this site we draw the horizontal line labeled "Wage Line." Wage, here, means the returns to *both* capital *and* labor. Everything above the margin of production goes to rent, and capital and labor divide what is left as best they can.

The law of rents does not work automatically, but is a tendency over time. At any given time, renters will be earning over the wage line, but increases in rent will erode their earnings. Over time, the margin of production will serve as the ceiling for wages and the floor for rents. How does this work? Let us say that you rent a parcel of land at one price and then improve its productivity; your earnings in this case will exceed the wage line. When it comes time to renew the lease, however, the landlord will demand a higher rent, since the property is now more productive; it has moved to the left on the horizontal axis. Since the land is more productive, someone will be willing to pay the increased rent, so you must either agree to pay or agree to move on.

Changes in Productivity

The unusual thing in the above example is that there is an increase in the rent even though there was no increase in demand. The landlord can demand a higher price for improvements made by the tenant. The increased profit was earned by the renter, but received (eventually) by the landlord. This is not an anomaly; it is simply the way land works in a system of concentrated land ownership. Let us examine the ways in which land may increase in value. There are basically three ways:

- an increase in population,
- an improvement in technology which makes land more productive, and
- off-site improvements, such as roads, utilities, buildings on other sites, etc.

An increase in population will, of course, mean more competition for land. It will also mean improved productivity for any given parcel of land. For example, if you operate a restaurant in an area where the population is increasing, you have a larger pool of potential customers to draw on, and the productivity of the property increases. So will the rent. Note that the increase in population is not something the landlord does (even if he is extremely prolific) but something the community does. *Nevertheless, the landlord reaps the reward.*

Improvements in technology, whether the moldboard plow in the tenth century or the Internet in the twentieth, increase the productivity of land. Initially, the benefits of these improvements will go to the user of the land, but eventually they find their way into the rent and hence into the pocket of the landlord. Note that these improvements are not something the landlord does, but something the community does. *Nevertheless, the landlord reaps the rewards.*

If the state builds a road adjacent to your property, the value of that property increases. The same is true for any off-site improvement. If your neighbor builds a large building on his piece of ground, the value of your piece of ground is likely to go up. In general, if you buy a piece of vacant ground, and a community grows up around it, the value of your land will increase without you having to do anything. Note that this growth is not something the landlord does, but something the community does. *Nevertheless, the landlord reaps the rewards.*

What is common to all three cases is that *the community does the work, but the landlord reaps the rewards.* This leads to the question of exactly what the social function of the landlord is. We know well what the worker contributes to society, and what the entrepreneur contributes, and what capital contributes. These groups make all the things that are made by man, but land is not made by man and exists quite independently of the landlord. Therefore, we may ask: "What function does the landlord perform, to reap such rich rewards from the labor of others?" One implication of this is that if the worker is to reap the full value of his labor, then he must own an interest in the land he works. This is of course a moral issue, but it is also an economic one. What the landlord gets is wealth without work, which means that somebody else must perform work without wealth. In such conditions, it is very difficult to achieve equilibrium by economic means, and we are forced to call upon the government and the usurers to balance demand.

This also explains why land, in any place where the population is increasing, will always be the best investment. There will be seasonal ups and downs in the price of land, but the secular trend will always be up so long as the population is increasing. But these seasonal adjustments are themselves a cause of great dislocations in an economy. To see how this works, let us return to the first chart in this chapter.

The Speculative Rent Line

When we look at this chart, we see that any increase in demand for land means that we have to establish a new demand curve, D_1, with a new rent line, R_1. The immediate cause of the increase in demand is likely an expansion of business activity. But there is also another line on the chart, D_2, and another rent line, SRL or the speculative rent line. The reason for this is that land is priced differently from real commodities. When you buy a real commodity, say a loaf of bread, the price reflects its history, that is, all the costs that went into making up the product, including the profit of the firm selling the bread. When you buy an income-producing instrument, however, say a share of stock or a bond, the price reflects not its past but its future. The price of such instruments reflects the buyer's estimate of the future cash flows associated with that instrument. The seller of a share of stock in Microsoft makes a guess as to the future growth and cash flows from the share, discounts these cash flows for the effects of inflation and his time-preference[3] for a return, and sets a price. If he finds a buyer with equal or greater expectations, he will sell the share. The buyer for his part makes the same guesses and calculations, and if he finds a seller with equal or lower expectations, he will buy the share. Note here that both parties are speculators making guesses in opposite directions, one a "bear" and the other a "bull."

What is evident about this transaction is that one party will be right and the other wrong. Microsoft may double in price next year, or it may disappear from the face of the earth, or, more likely, suffer some fate in-between; one party will have guessed well and the other badly. In the same way, the deed to a parcel of land is also an income-producing instrument, priced by its future rather than by its past. But land is not like other equities. Both the buyer and seller understand that the price is likely to rise in the long-term, so long as the population continues to increase. What is at issue between the buyer and seller is not the eventual value, but the timeframe and discount rate. Both buyer and seller are long-term bulls, even if they are short-term bears. This tends to put an upward speculative pressure on land prices. In equities, speculation tends to work in both directions, and hence balances itself out, over time. But in land, speculation tends to work in one direction only, at least in the long-term.

This puts a near-constant upward pressure on rents. Landowners add to this pressure by withholding their land from the market. If you look around an American city, you will see, once you pass the older core of the city, an alteration of developed and undeveloped or under-developed parcels. The un- and under-developed parcels are where owners are holding land off the market in expectation of a better price, in the confidence that, sooner or later, the market must rise to meet their price. This withholding of land further restricts supply, and hence becomes a self-fulfilling prophecy. As long as the costs of withholding land are low, owners can keep doing so to their advantage. Thus the land market, instead of finding equilibrium at R_1, tends to exceed the equilibrium price and rise towards the speculative rent line. When we recall that rents can only increase at the expense of wages and profits, we realize that this is not a socially neutral process. The rising rents attract more investment and more speculation, until a speculative bubble develops. During this bubble, money that could be used for investment is misdirected to mere speculation. Investment is the serious job of providing firms with the funds necessary to expand production and hiring. Speculation is merely a bet on the direction of an asset, without providing any funds for business expansion. As the bubble grows, banks lend money to speculators to buy more land, and to landowners based on the inflated values of their land. The added credit works like pouring gasoline on a fire, fueling the frenzy and driving the rent line higher and higher—and consequently depressing the wage line.[4]

All of this speculation constricts business activity. It acts like a tax on profits and wages, depressing the real market for goods and services.

The bubble, of course, cannot continue forever. The rising rent chokes off the business activity that was the original impetus for the increase in the demand for land. Suddenly, the bubble bursts, land values collapse, and lenders who borrowed in expectation of rising land prices cannot repay their loans. Banks restrict credit or go under entirely. Businesses find credit hard to come by, and further restrict their hiring, or even let employees go. All of this happens not because there is a lack of some necessary thing in the economy. On the contrary, there is land to work, hands to work on it, and tools enough to work with. There is the desire for goods, and the desire to supply those goods. There is a willingness to work—even at depressed wages—and more than enough work that needs to be done. Nevertheless, land lies vacant, hands lie idle, and capital finds no investment.

The collapse wipes out all the bad debts and readjusts the rent line back to a sustainable level, and the cycle begins again. But one wonders if such a cycle is an inevitable part of business, or whether it is something we have done to ourselves because we misunderstand economic reality, and have treated things which are not commodities as if they were. We can also note that these cycles are intolerable to both workers and businesses alike, and are always accompanied by the call for government to "do something." And the government usually does. Further, the government has done fairly well over the last sixty years (see chapter 2). The cycles of this period have been milder than at any time in capitalism's history, but one wonders if this federal remedy can heal the economy forever. Each new crisis seems to demand greater effort—and greater debts. We come to a point, I believe, when the government can do nothing further, and everything it can do serves only to make the problem worse. But if government can do nothing further for us, is there something further we can do for ourselves? Answering this question forms the burden of the remainder of this book.

10

Property as Proper to Man

Crimes Against Nature

We have thus far identified the fictitious commodities as those things which do not have a commodity-like supply and demand chart. That is, supply and demand are not brought into balance by the price. Insofar as modern economic science is dependent on such a balance, it must leave out the three most important factors of economic order: labor, land, and money. Thus, insofar as modern theory is dependent upon fictitious commodities it must be a fictitious theory and can never be scientific in any sense of that term. The best it can do is science fiction. And if I am going to read science fiction, I prefer Heinlein to Friedman; the economics is the same but the writing is better.

The failure of land, labor, and money to function as commodities, however, is only part of the problem. Land and labor are just alternate names for nature and man. Fictionalizing these commodities leaves out their most important values, values which are critical not only in a moral sense, but in an economic sense as well. Fictionalizing these natural things distorts their natures by reducing them to a pure utility, with

113

"utility" distorted to mean "the ability to earn a profit for its owner." And indeed, property does have utility of this kind, but it has other utilities as well, and when we ignore them, we violate its true nature. When we violate the true nature of a thing, we strip it of any real utility. For example, if we turn the river into a sewer, we find that we can no longer use it as a river and soon won't be able to use it as a sewer. It is quite true that some people did get rich by using the rivers as sewers, but this is not real wealth, merely a reappropriation of public resource to private benefit. Now, a river is, of course, a natural sewer, designed to carry off and process certain kinds of naturally occurring waste at certain volumes. Any proper use of the river must be in accord with the nature of the river. Wastes from a factory must be reduced to the kinds and volumes that the river is capable of handling. To do otherwise is to commit a crime against nature. Modern economics simply institutionalizes these crimes.

Wealth and Property

All wealth creation occurs at the intersection of man and nature. Only by applying human labor to the gifts of nature can any wealth be created. Therefore, if we wish to reconstruct political economy on scientific grounds, we must start with a proper accounting of man and nature, and of the relationship between them. This relationship we call "property." Property relations are the most basic of all economic and social relationships. Property relations determine all other economic outcomes. If property is gathered into a few hands, then few will have any real claim on wealth. If one kind of property is privileged over another, then all other property claimants will have to reduce their claims.

Of course, all men and women have some property. Indeed, it is impossible to be a man without ownership of at least some food, clothing, and shelter. If a man has no property in these, he ceases to be a man and will soon cease to be at all. In political economy, what we are most concerned with is property in things that can be used to produce other things, that is to say, the means of production. From what we have said so far, these means are basically two, with a third that arises from both. The first kind is the property a man has in himself and his labor, including his education, skill, dedication, etc. The second kind is the property a man has in natural things, most prominently land, but also things like airwaves and the food, fiber, and mineral wealth that comes from the land. From these two, there is a third kind of property, the man-made tools that are used to produce more things, commonly called "capital." Who owns these things, and what rights each owner has, will be the sole determinant of economic outcomes.

Despite this primacy of property relations in economics, property gets very little space in modern economics. It is regarded as an unproblematic and simple notion about which the only debate is whether it will be privately owned or controlled by officers of the state. This public-or-private debate is actually no debate at all, especially since the fall of economies that actually attempted pure public ownership. Hence real inquiry into the nature and duties of property has been short-circuited and banished from economics to the world of philosophers and theologians. The issues do belong to those realms, but they are properly economic issues as well. And the properly economic inquiry proceeds along these lines: the origins of ownership and the relationship between ownership and use, along with the question of whose claims are superior, the owner's or the user's.

The Origins of Ownership

The question of the origins of ownership is referred often to prehistory, that poorly documented period about which people may make any number of claims without actually having to—or being able to—verify them. This is not necessary, however, since new forms of property are being created today, property with claims whose origins we can easily examine, and about which we can make judgments. For example, there are new property rights in the use of the airwaves or in ocean drilling rights. We have seen even the creation of a property right to pollute in the so-called cap and trade systems, a form of property which is nothing less than the right to poison your neighbor. A radio or TV station, for example, must have exclusive use of some particular radio frequency and hence must have a property in that frequency. Where does this claim come from? Quite simply, the government gives it to the broadcaster. Bits of the airwaves are given to private owners for their use and enjoyment, and public claims are extinguished or diluted. Sometimes there is a charge, say a lease agreement, and sometimes it is a pure gift of the government.

We live in an age when even "democratic" governments have near totalitarian powers. Nevertheless, there are lessons to be drawn from their property-creation actions which apply to property in any situation. The first lesson is that property is originally communal (owned by the community) and granted to individuals. Indeed, the very idea of a purely private property is a contradiction in terms, since the right to private property must be recognized by the community to have any value. For example, the owner must be able to call upon the police to exclude others from his property, or his property cannot be said to be private at all. This fact led Adam Smith to conclude that government "is in reality instituted for the defense of the rich against the poor, or of those who have some property against those who have none at all."[1] We here ignore the question of whether that is what government *ought* to be, and merely note that in the case of property, that is what it *must* be. If I cannot call the police to evict the invader from my living room, I cannot actually be said to own my own home; my private claim depends on public authority. Indeed, if my claim to private property is to be absolute, then the police powers of the state must also be absolute, or at least absolute with regard to property claims.

This leads to the question of how the community (which in our present state of affairs means the state) ought to allocate property. The most common method is by original use. When, for example, the pioneer goes beyond the margin of civilization and breaks the soil on virgin land, the state ought to recognize his claim to ownership. This claim is based on what we might call *natural property,* that is, the property a person has in himself and his own labor, a right which is self-evident and reducible to nothing else. Furthermore, each person has a natural title to whatever his labor produces. A person who makes something is considered the owner of that thing, to the extent that the labor and the materials are his.

Ownership and Use

Ownership is related to first *use.* Usage and ownership in this case are united, and the state ought to recognize the user as the owner. What we might call the natural title precedes the conventional or legal title. But what happens when the pioneer breaks the virgin soil and makes it productive, only to find out that someone, perhaps the King of Spain, has already granted a legal title to some hidalgo, a lord who now demands an economic rent from the pioneer? In this case, ownership and usage are separated, with legal ownership preceding natural ownership. It is this division between ownership and usage that causes all the interesting problems of private property.

The classical position on the relationship of ownership and use is given by Thomas Aquinas. For Aquinas, there is no particular reason why a "particular piece of land should belong to one man more than another."[2] Nevertheless, Aquinas gives an excellent defense of private property:

> [Private property] is necessary to human life for three reasons. First because every man is more careful to procure what is for himself alone than that which is common to many or to all: since each one would shirk the labor and leave to another that which concerns the community, as happens where there is a great number of servants. Secondly, because human affairs are conducted in more orderly fashion if each man is charged with taking care of some particular thing himself, whereas there would be confusion if everyone had to look after any one thing indeterminately. Thirdly, because a more peaceful state is ensured to man if each one is contented with his own. Hence it is to be observed that quarrels arise more frequently where there is no division of things possessed.[3]

The thing to note about this defense is that it is *pragmatic:* things just work better when there is private ownership. But then Aquinas identifies a second aspect of property, its use. He writes:

> The second thing that is competent to man with regard to external things is their use. In this respect man ought to possess external things, not as his own, but as common, so that, to wit, he is ready to communicate them to others in their need.[4]

Thus Aquinas identifies two aspects of property: *ownership* and *use.* One dictates a *private* aspect of property and the other a *public* or *common* aspect. What is the relationship between these two aspects? As Aquinas says,

Community of goods is ascribed to the natural law, not that the natural law dictates that all things should be possessed in common and that nothing should be possessed as one's own: but because the division of possessions is not according to the natural law, but rather arose out of human agreement which belongs to the positive law . . . Hence the ownership of possessions is not contrary to the natural law, but an addition thereto devised by human reason.[5]

Indeed, the common claims on property are so strong that theft is allowed in cases of need: "In cases of need all things are common property, so that there would seem to be no sin in taking another's property, for need has made it common."[6]

For Aquinas, then, there is a common aspect of property that is governed by the natural law and a private aspect that is governed by positive law, or prudence. Now we can better understand Aquinas's pragmatic defense of private property: it is a method, governed only by prudence, of insuring that the natural, common values of property will be available to all; it is a way to ensure that property will be properly developed so as to be useful to the whole community, since property always needs to be developed in some sense in order that its values be made available to men. Private property is therefore a means to an end. But what happens when such property no longer fulfills this end, and even works contrary to it? Is such property still legitimate?

The Misuse of Property

In the case where the owner and the user are the same person, few issues arise in private property. But what happens when the owner and the user are different persons? What happens when the hidalgo demands from the pioneer a share in the grain he did not grow? The hidalgo's share is not related to any work the hidalgo does, other than the work of bullying the pioneer. This is, of course, a moral issue. It is, therefore, an economic issue. Economic equilibrium depends on each person getting the wealth he creates, while disequilibrium is caused by wealth without work, by those who do no work but claim the output from others who do work. What does the hidalgo in this case produce? Nothing. His entire economic function is to reduce the pioneer to penury, an action sure to discourage the pioneering spirit.

The hidalgo has a perfect right to charge for any services he provides to the property. If he clears a road to it, or digs a well, or builds a house, he may with justice charge the pioneer for these things. His own labor and capital have the same right to a return as do the labor and capital of the pioneer. But without providing anything, what is the moral basis of his claim? The legal basis is clear enough: his grant from the king of Spain. The police powers of the state are used to extract a rent from the pioneer to the hidalgo. But while this is legally defensible, it is economic nonsense. Or more technically, it is *economic rent*.

Economic rent is an amount paid to a factor of production that is more than necessary to keep that factor in production in its current use. It is the very essence of economic inefficiency. For example, the price of steel must be enough to pay for the raw materials in the steel and to compensate the labor and capital that went into making it. If, however, the price rises very much above this amount, then steel claims an economic rent. This rent acts like a tax on all users of the steel, a tax that really doesn't buy anything, but only transfers money from one group (the consumers) to another (the owners). In the case of elastic, reproducible commodities (like steel), this is only a short-term problem, since (in competitive markets) the higher prices attract more labor and capital, the supply is increased, the prices fall, and the economic rent disappears. But this does not happen in the case of property. The rent is chronic and distorts the returns to both capital and labor.

Land always collects an economic rent. The landlord provides no services to the land for which he can make a legitimate charge (again, keep in mind we are talking about the ground rent, and not any improvements the landlord might make to the land). The land does not depreciate, hence there can be no depreciation expense. Any gains in the price of the land are attributable not to the landlord, but to the community. Owning land provides no value to the land; only its use can provide value to the community. Nevertheless, the landlord collects a rent which must be regarded as an economic rent.

Private property can be misused in another way: it can be *not* used at all, but held for mere speculative purposes, or to prevent others from using it. As an example of the latter, there is, as I write this, a great debate going on about offshore drilling leases. There is, however, an air of unreality about this debate, since the oil companies already have huge offshore oil leases that they could drill tomorrow; indeed, the number of drilling rights they have but do not use is several times greater than the leases they are seeking. So why seek them? They are not sought for purposes of drilling, but for purposes of control. By controlling the leases, they can insure that nobody else drills. There is a perverse incentive to do this. Oil costs perhaps $10–20 per barrel to bring to the surface, but sells (as of this writing) for $86 per barrel. Further drilling would only raise the supply and lower the price. Why should they drill now, if they control the rights? The oil is not going anywhere, and they can drill it in some distant tomorrow when their current fields run out. In this way, they can control the price, collect a huge economic rent, and guarantee that they do so far into the future. Of course, the answer here is obvious: make the leases a "use-it-or-lose-it" proposition. Any oil company can have any lease wherever they like, but they must use it within a few years or it reverts to public ownership and can be re-leased to someone who will actually use it. This "use-it-or-lose-it" approach can be applied to any property. Property that cannot be used is held by the public until it can be sold to someone who can make it productive. There is in fact an easy (and tested) way to do this, which we will discuss in the chapter on taxation.

Property as Sacred

Note that none of this can be construed as an argument against private property. Such property is natural to man. It is as natural for a man to say, "This is *my* book," or "This is *my* home," as it is for him to breathe. But if a comparatively few people can say of the bulk of productive property, "This is mine," it must mean that the bulk of mankind cannot make the same statement. They will be, therefore, at the mercy of those who own productive property, and will exist by their leave and on such terms as they will allow. Property acquires a sacred nature when it is associated with labor, and serves as the guarantee that the laborer will get his just reward and not pay an economic rent for the privilege of living. Property is the guarantee that the worker and the investor will get their just rewards. As such, it will be the means to eliminate economic rents and to establish the economy on a sane, equitable, and workable basis.

We do not posit this as some idle dream. Instead, we point to systems where the workers do own the means of production: employee owned enterprises around the world, and firms like the Mondragón Cooperative, where eightythousand worker-owners control their own destinies by their own labor. In Mondragón, the workers have built not only successful enterprises, but a whole social safety net and educational system. Further, they have built this system from their own earnings, without recourse to the taxing power of the state. We will cover Mondragón and similar enterprises in a later chapter; for now it is enough to know that we are speaking of actually existing systems, and not some utopian pipe dream.

Property must be seen as an aid to productive work, and not a substitute for it. When ownership and use are separated, a class that has claims to wealth without work is created, which means there must be another (and larger) class that works without wealth. This accumulation of property into the hands of those who do not use it is the sole cause of the vast inequalities that bedevil civil society and economic order, as Adam Smith recognized:

> Wherever there is great property there is great inequality. For one very rich man there must be at least five hundred poor, and the affluence of the few supposes the indigence of the many. The affluence of the rich excites the indignation of the poor, who are often both driven by want, and prompted by envy, to invade his possessions. It is only under the shelter of the civil magistrate that the owner of that valuable property . . . can sleep a single night in security.[7]

Some will, no doubt, see in this attempt to limit property an attack on property. But this is not so, for every proper right has its own proper limit. As G. K. Chesterton put it:

> I am well aware that the word "property" has been defied in our time by the corruption of the great capitalists. One would think, to hear people talk, that the Rothchilds and the Rockefellers were on the side of property. But obviously they are the enemies of property; because they are enemies of their own limitations. . . . It is the negation of property that the Duke

of Sutherland should have all the farms in one estate; just as it would be the negation of marriage if he had all our wives in one harem.[8]

Or as Calvin was reported to have said, "Wealth is like manure; it works best when it is spread, but stinks when it is in one big pile."

11

The Just Wage as
the Key to Equilibrium

The Return to Reality

It should be obvious that a scientific economics cannot be built upon fictitious commodities. Things that, manifestly, are not commodities—do not respond to supply and demand curves, and are not elastic—cannot be treated as commodities. Mostly, the economy cannot be reduced to a series of exchanges to eliminate the need for distributive justice. Economics cannot be made a science along the lines of physics, where everything can be reduced to number, but is a humane science, one that requires humane considerations.

But if we are to return economics to a more realistic base, which path should we follow? Three broad paths have been suggested by various schools of thought, each one of which tends to concentrate on reform of one of the fictitious commodities. The Georgists would reform our understanding of land, the institutionalists would reform our understanding of labor, and the followers of Major Douglas and other monetary reformers would reform the banks and eliminate usury. Which of these paths should a proper reform take? The answer is, "All of the above." That is, you can start from any of these positions, and as long as you reach out to and include the other positions, you will end in roughly the same place. And that place will be a lot closer to reality—will be more scientific—than anything neoclassical or Austrian economics has to offer.

What unites all three of these approaches is that they all embody, explicitly or implicitly, some notion of distributive justice. The Georgists would reclaim the values of land that are produced by the community and redistribute them to the community that produced them; the institutionalists would ensure that the worker gets a just proportion of what he produces; the monetary reformers would eliminate usury, that is, fortunes that are based not on producing any useful goods or services but instead appropriate, through financial manipulation, the wealth produced by others. But is there a term which unites and includes all three sets of reforms? I suggest that there is. This term is the "just wage." The just wage involves the idea of the proportionality of rewards that lies at the heart of distributive justice, and depends for its implementation on a reform of the notions of property and the elimination of usury.

Although "just wage" is the more common term, we could as easily call it "just returns" and thereby include the returns to capital, since capital is labor in another form. Or it could be called the "just price," as it was by the Scholastic economists, since a price includes the just rewards to both labor and capital *and* eliminates any economic rents (wealth without work). But in its modern form, it is known as the "just wage," and the idea originates not from within economics, but with a priest, Leo XIII, the pontiff of the Roman Catholic Church. He wrote his teaching in the encyclical *Rerum Novarum* ("Of New Things") in 1891.

A Scandalous Encyclical?

Leo XIII described the "new things" this way: it "gradually came about that the present age handed over the workers, each alone and defenseless, to the inhumanity of employers and the unbridled greed of competitors . . . so that a very few rich and exceedingly rich men have laid a yoke almost of slavery on the unnumbered masses of non-owning workers."[1] This is a densely packed sentence, focusing on the inhumanity and greed that made the mass of humanity into virtual slaves, and its tone would have pleased even Karl Marx. Nevertheless, the encyclical as a whole was a largely conservative document. Leo upholds private property as a sacred right; he is suspicious of unions; he condemns Socialism outright and in very round terms; he condemns the call to revolutionary and violent action. On the other hand, Leo has a revolutionary call of his own. In making the just wage the linchpin of Catholic social teaching, the encyclical began a controversy which continues to this day.

Just what is this "just wage"? Leo defines it as an amount sufficient to support a "thrifty and upright" worker and his family without having to put his wife and children out to work at paid labor.[2] Furthermore, the wage must be sufficient to allow a thrifty worker to save and acquire some property of his own.[3] By this means, says the pope, there will be a more equitable division of goods, and the differences between the classes will be lessened.[4] Leo makes no attempt to justify his views in economic terms. He does not situate his just wage requirement in any economic theory. Rather, he advances it as a purely moral requirement of the economy, and leaves it to the economists to work out the theoretical details.

But the just wage is exactly the sort of moral entanglement that the economists were seeking to avoid. *Rerum Novarum* came at the precise moment when economists believed that they had reduced all economic questions to a science of free exchanges, a science that eliminated all questions of distributive justice. Now, either Leo's encyclical constituted a scandalous religious interference in the affairs of science, comparable to the Galileo affair, or else the pope had located the flaw in the (then) new economics. So had the pope overstepped his competence and his authority? To judge that, we will have to look at how the new economics treated wages.

The Neoclassical Theory of Wages (and Everything Else)

In Leo's day, economists were working on several varieties of equilibrium theory, all of which reduced wages to a question of "free" exchanges. One of the best known formulations of the theory comes from J. B. Clark's *The Distribution of Wealth,* published in 1899, just eight years after the publication of *Rerum Novarum.* According to Clark, both wages and profit are allocated by a "deep-acting natural law":[5]

> *Where natural laws have their way, the share of income that attaches to any productive function is gauged by the actual product of [that function].* In other words, free competition tends to give labor what labor creates, to capitalists what capital creates, and to *entrepreneurs* what the coordinating function creates.[6]

Clark asserted that the "natural" wage of labor was the return an employer could get on the "marginal man," that is, the last man that could be profitably hired. In explicating this iron law, the task for Clark was to show that the marginal wage, the wage of the least productive person represented the "specific product of labor," and of labor alone.[7]

Clark reasoned that this "marginal man" could be hired "with no change in the amount or character of capital goods."[8] Therefore, the amount he added to production—and this amount alone—was the only part of production attributable to labor alone and constituted the "specific product of labor." Labor was therefore entitled by "natural law" only to this part of the produce. Clark made no attempt to fix the "specific product of capital"; he merely assumed it was the whole product minus the wages.[9]

Clark believed that the forces of free competition would force prices to equal the cost of production, driving the rate of profit to zero, so that the entrepreneur would earn little more than the worker.[10] In other words, wages and profits would be normalized to each other, with the capitalist earning roughly what the worker did; there would neither be great wealth nor great poverty. The productivity of both capital and labor would be fairly rewarded, and rewards for each would change at a rate exactly corresponding to the rate of the change in productivity.

Critique of Clark's Theory

The simplest critique of Clark's theory is that we have never seen it in practice. Returns to wages and capital in a capitalist society do not seem to be normalized to each other, nor do they seem to be well related to productivity. For example, productivity for all classes of labor has exploded in the last forty years, yet the real wage of the median worker has stagnated; he or she simply has not gotten any real gains from the real gains in productivity. At the same time, wages at the top of the scale, the upper executive level, have exploded. The executives have gained all that the worker and the investor have lost. Yet there seems to be little empirical evidence that these high salaries are related to their productivity, since they seem to make the same high salaries whether they drive the company up or down.

The defenders of neoclassical equilibrium theories might sidestep this critique by pointing out that the theory depends on a perfectly free market, a market that does not in fact exist. Therefore, there can be no empirical confirmation or refutation of the theory. For the moment, we'll ignore the obvious flaws in that line of thinking and accept the defense for the sake of argument and critique the theory on its own grounds.

The first problem that we notice is that the procedure Clark used is arbitrary. He attempted to figure the "marginal productivity" of the last man employed and then merely *assumed* that capital gets all the rest. But why not reverse the procedure? Why not figure the marginal productivity of the last dollar employed and assume that labor gets all the rest? Either procedure would be equally valid.

Or rather, each would be equally invalid. The theory tries to figure the "independent productivity" of capital and labor, but this number is in fact the only precisely known number in all of economics: it is precisely zero. Neither capital nor labor produces anything without the other. The proof is simple. Take any item of capital, a truck let us say, and watch it all day to see what values it produces by itself. It will produce none, unless and until a driver mounts the cab to make some pickups and deliveries. Independent productivities are a mythical quantity, which is why they have never been empirically measured; you may as well attempt to measure the wingspan of a gryphon or the height of a dragon. Capital without labor is sterile, and labor without capital is simply another name for unemployment. Production is a social process, occurring only at the intersection of land, labor, and capital. The productivity of a given process may be reliably measured and compared with other production processes, but the productivity of factors within the process cannot be reliably measured; one can only make a judgment about them, a judgment that cannot be reduced to mathematics.

Nor is there any reason to believe that wage contracts and free bargaining would fairly reward actual productivity. Indeed, Adam Smith had debunked this argument more than one hundred years before Clark made it. Concerning labor negotiations, Smith said,

> It is not, however, difficult to foresee which of the two parties must, upon all ordinary occasions, have the advantage in the dispute, and force the other into a compliance with their terms. . . . A landlord, a farmer, a master manufacturer, a merchant, though they did not employ a single workman, could generally live a year or two upon the stocks which they have already acquired. Many workmen could not subsist a week, few could subsist a month, and scarce any a year without employment. In the long run the workman may be as necessary to his master as his master is to him; but the necessity is not so immediate.[11]

In other words, negotiations tend to be about power, not productivity. This is true of contract negotiations in general, which always tend to give the stronger party the better deal. In a capitalist society, and absent strong laws, functioning labor unions, or ready alternatives to the jobs offered, capital tends to have more negotiating power than labor, and hence tends to get a larger share of the rewards. When this happens, as it usually does, capital tends to be overcompensated. Capital then accumulates faster than wages, while the broad consumer market narrows, meaning there is less real investment opportunity for the oversupplied capital. At this point, economic equilibrium is impossible, and the economy must rely on the noneconomic means of balancing supply and demand, that is, on charity, welfare, and usury.

The Wage Contract

Having said all that, we could *wish* that Clark was right. We could rightly wish that free bargaining alone was enough to establish a just wage, while also ensuring a just return in an environment of just prices—that is, prices that do not produce an economic rent. We could wish that there was a way to overcome Smith's objection and balance the negotiating power between the parties. The question that has to be dealt with is not productivity, but power. Increasing the productivity of the worker has not, in the real world, led to an increase in his wage. But increasing his power nearly always does. So if we want Clark's vision of a link between productivity and wages, we will have to balance the negotiating power of the worker and the employer. As a methodological point, whenever we are dealing with practical problems, it is always a good idea to look at the real world and see what alternatives exist and how well they work. Economists and others are often trapped in theories that are poorly related to real-world conditions, an intellectual disease they could cure by simply looking up from their books now and then and seeing how the real world works. So, has the negotiating power of the worker and the employer ever been balanced successfully? Yes. There are three methods: strong laws, strong unions, and the distribution of property.

Strong Laws

For the last one hundred years Australia has had a method of setting wages by a system of special courts.[12] Sweden and New Zealand have had similar systems. These courts operate independently of the government, and they encourage the parties to work out their differences without coming to the courts. The mere existence of the courts is usually sufficient to get the parties to agree, since both sides understand the rules by which the court will make its decisions.

The economies that use this system tend to have highly productive workforces and relatively stable economies. Opponents of the system argue that it reduces incentives to work, but this is not borne out by the facts. The mere existence of this system, and its long-standing success, is sufficient refutation of the idea that wages are best set by a free-market system.

Nevertheless, the Australian system, and others like it, have exhibited problems from time to time. The system is highly dependent on unions, which has both strengths and weaknesses. These systems also increase the power of the state and may forestall necessary reforms in other areas, such as banking and land ownership. Still, it is an option that, because of its persistent success, deserves careful attention.

Strong Unions

When the unions were strong in the United States, wage rates were higher. Most men were able to earn a decent living without putting their wives to work. The truth is that when labor is united, it turns out to be much stronger than capital. However, this very strength turns out to be labor's greatest weakness. Labor unions often ask for too much, and because of their inherent power, they get it. The problem with unions is that they institutionalize the division between capital and labor, just as much as the corporation does. Unions, in fact, tend to be mere mirror images of the corporations on the other side of the table, each seeking its own ends but using the same methods. But the sign of a successful labor system is that it overcomes this opposition. Capital, after all, is just "stored-up labor" and its rights and rewards spring from the same source.

A perfect example of the problems with unions is the labor contracts reached with the auto industry in the 1970s. These were nothing more than mutual suicide pacts, by which labor got more than the companies could possibly give without damaging their viability. Eventually, the system had to come to an end, with catastrophic consequences for both sides.

Moreover, it is incorrect to talk about a united labor movement, because divisions within the movement can be greater than their divisions with the companies. For example, the interests of unions of skilled workers can be contrary to the interests of the unskilled workers, and since the skilled workers have greater bargaining power, they can get privileges that come at the expense of other workers.

This is not to be taken as an argument against unions per se. It is, however, an argument against a divisive labor movement, divided within itself and against capital. What is required is a strong sense of solidarity, not only with all other workers, unionized or not, but with the poor, and even with capital itself—in other words, what is needed is a commitment to the common good, not the particular interest. The unions must take responsibility not only for the welfare of the workers, but for the welfare of the firm as well, since the two are mutually dependent. Management, for its part, aids this solidarity by practicing open-book management, that is, by giving all the members of the firm access to the books. Only in this way can all members of the firm—workers, managers, and owners—be assured that decisions are being made with the common good in mind. As Pope John Paul II pointed out, "A labour system can be right . . . in the sense of being intrinsically true and also morally legitimate, if in its very basis *it overcomes the opposition between labour and capital*."[13]

The Distribution of Property

The simplest way to overcome the opposition between capital and labor is simply to dissolve the difference between the two, to make the workers the owners of the capital they create. Our current system erects a high wall between the owners of capital and the workers, and allocates all rewards above the wage to capital. Yet this system is neither necessary nor natural. The current system makes good Clark's assumption that everything earned above the lowest possible wage belongs to capital. And certainly, there would be no production without capital. But neither would there be any use for capital without labor.

Nor is the current system particularly efficient. In fact, it creates huge dis-economies in the form of *agency costs*. Agency costs are incurred when one party acts as the agent for another. In such contracts, there are rewards and sanctions to encourage the agents to act in the best interests of the principals. But the agents may have their own agendas and take their own interests to heart more than those of the owners they are supposed to serve. According to John Bogle, the founder and former CEO of the Vanguard Funds, a large mutual fund company, this is exactly what has happened today, with the upper echelons of management taking an inordinate share of the rewards to the detriment of both capital and labor:

> Over the past century, a gradual move from *owners' capitalism*—providing the lion's share of the rewards of investment to those who put up the money and risk their own capital—has culminated in an extreme version of *manager's capitalism*—providing vastly disproportionate rewards to those whom we have trusted to manage our enterprises in the interest of the owners. [14]

When owners and workers are the same persons, these inefficiencies tend to disappear, which gives worker-owned firms a competitive advantage over their more capitalistic and agency-ridden counterparts, a point we will examine in more detail later on.

When people hear "distribution of property," many automatically think, "Socialism!" But nothing could be further from the truth. In a capitalist system, there are few owners of the means of production, but in a socialist system, there is only one, the state. Socialism, in fact, forms sort of a natural terminus for a capitalistic system, as the interests of the state bureaucrats and the corporate bureaucrats tend to converge. Historically, both bureaucracies wax fat together, rather than one being a check on the other. But in a distributed system of property, there are many owners. Ownership becomes the "natural" condition of people in that society. When workers have access to their own tools, land, and capital, the problems of unfair labor contracts are overcome. A mechanic, for example, who owns his own tools and his own land can evaluate any offer of employment he receives against the money he can make by himself and the freedom of movement that he has, and make a decision as to whether the offer is in his and his family's best interest. The compulsion of the labor contract, the problem that Adam Smith pointed out, disappears.

As for the mechanics of the distribution of property, we have many successful examples to go by, including the "land to the tiller" programs of Taiwan and Korea, the Georgist policies of Singapore and other places, the Mondragón Cooperative Corporation, and thousands of successful Employee Stock Ownership Plans. We will examine these methods in a later chapter; for now, it is enough to say that we know the problems can be overcome (and relatively easily) because they have been overcome.

The Just Wage and Equilibrium

The just wage represents people taking out of the system in consumption no more than they put in by production. This, by definition, constitutes equilibrium. But how do we know that just wages are those wages which will support a family? Directly, we don't. But indirectly, we do, because the contrary proposition is absurd. If we assert that wages in general should not support the family, then economics becomes an absurd science with no real purpose. If economic systems in general just don't work, then we must choose between chaos or Keynesianism. To have a sane economy, that is, an economic system that fulfills its economic purposes, you must have either distributive justice, as in distributism, or re-distributive justice, as in Keynesianism.

The entire economic problem always comes down to a question of wealth without work. If you have people with vast incomes who produce little, then you must have people who produce much but get little income. This wealth without work is economic rent, and it comes in many forms: ground rents, speculation, usury, the looting of companies by the executive class, etc.

The reader will note that I have not stated a number for the just wage. This is because the just wage is not really a number at all. Rather, it is a standard of judgment. It is impossible to give a generalized number for the just wage because it will vary from place to place, time to time, and culture to culture. Further, even in any specific setting, there are just too many jobs, companies, and specifics to set a number on the just wage. Nor should we set a specific number. Rather, we can judge that the just wage is fulfilled under the following four conditions: one, that working families, as a rule, appear to live in the dignity appropriate for that society; two, that they can do so without putting wives and children to work; three, that they have some security against periods of enforced unemployment, such as sickness, layoffs, and old age; and, four, that these conditions are accomplished without undue reliance on welfare payments and usury. While it may be difficult to give precision to any of these factors, it is certainly possible to make reasonable judgments and set reasonable standards.

12

Taxes and Tax Reform

The Fourth Factor

Thus far, we have been speaking of economics in terms of three factors of production: land, labor, and capital. This way of speaking has a long tradition in economics, but in fact there is a fourth factor: government. Production takes place within a framework of laws, institutions, and improvements such as roads, schools, airports, coinage, national defense, and courts. There are those who claim that these things can be provided apart from government. That may indeed be true, and for some things it must be true. Since it has never happened in all of human history, however, that all of these things were supplied apart from the government, we have no such systems to examine, and hence we can safely leave that argument to the higher realms of economic speculation, and concentrate on what actually occurs in the real world.

Are Taxes Theft?

Unfortunately, all of these things that government provides have a cost and need to be paid for. Typically, they are funded through taxation. Certain libertarians proclaim, "All taxes are theft." Perhaps, but the claims would have more force if libertarians would refuse to call the police when their homes have been robbed, or the fire department when their homes are burning. One could say that this holds the libertarian to too high a standard, since we must all live in the world as it is and obey its rules. But since we do live in the world, we must pay for the services we consume; this is not theft, it is simply being an adult.

Nevertheless, even if we cannot agree that *all* taxes are theft, we might agree that *most* taxes are, or at least are ill-considered, poorly administered, and unfair allocations of the burdens of government that negatively impact production, are expensive to administer, and intrude into the private life of citizens. All of these objections are valid. From both the Right and the Left, we have a near-unanimous consensus that *something* is wrong. Unfortunately, they cannot agree on just *what* is wrong. Reform proposals abound, but none have sufficient political support to gain any traction. The major disputes concern two issues: the progressive nature of taxes (whether those who make more should pay a proportionally higher rate) and the income from capital ought to be privileged over income from labor, or even whether such income should be taxed at all. On the Left, the principles of progressive taxation and the taxing of capital are generally agreed upon, and reform is simply a matter of adjusting the existing code to realize these principles more perfectly. But on the Right, there are at least two proposals which eliminate or seriously compromise the progressive nature of income taxes and reduce or eliminate taxes on capital income. These proposals are called the *flat tax* and the *fair tax*.

Examining these proposals will give us some insight into the nature of income taxes.

The Flat Tax

The flat tax replaces the current graduated tax rates with a single tax rate applied to all incomes. The rate is designed to be "revenue neutral," that is, to raise the same amount of money for the government that the current income tax does. If that were all it was, the debate would be confined to the question of whether taxes ought to be "progressive," that is, whether those with a higher income ought to pay a greater share of that income. Most flat-tax proposals, however, go far beyond this to radically redefine the very notions of income and cost accounting.

The flat tax would have a single rate, about 17 percent in most proposals, and also eliminate all deductions, except a standard deduction, about $12,000 for each adult and $6,000 for each child. Proponents of this plan say that all the complex tax forms can be reduced to two postcards, one for individual payers and another for businesses. The individual postcard would simply have a line for "income," a line for the standard deduction and another for the 17 percent tax rate. The business postcard would have a line for revenues, another for cost of goods sold, and any positive difference between the two would be taxed at 17 percent. The business taxes would exclude income from interest, dividends, rents, and capital gains. Proponents believe that they can get the nine-million-word tax code down to a few pages. It should be pointed out that the "postcard" form for individuals already exists, the 1040EZ, which although it is not printed on a postcard, could be and still remain legible.

The first problem with the flat tax is that it only replaces current income taxes, not the Social Security and Medicare taxes. These taxes come to 15.3 percent when the employer's contribution is considered. Therefore, the average worker will have all of his income taxed at 15.3 percent, and any amount over the standard deduction taxed at a total of 32.3 percent. This is close to the 35 percent currently paid by those with the highest incomes on the last portion of their income. Further, since the wealthy earn a higher proportion of their income from interest, dividends, rents, and capital gains, a large portion would not be taxed at all. The result would be a massive shifting of the tax burden from the rich to the middle class; people at the bottom would continue to pay the FICA taxes, as today, the people in the middle would have their total tax increased to 32.3 percent, and the rich would see their taxes substantially lowered or eliminated entirely. To put it another way, the rich will pay approximately what the middle class now pays, while the "middle class" (defined as anybody making more than the poverty level) will pay a marginal rate equal to what the rich now pay. And those among the rich whose income is completely from capital (dividends and interest) will see their taxes abolished entirely; they will be taxed as if they were desperately poor, at a 0 percent marginal rate.

Indeed, any "revenue neutral" scheme can only shift taxes, not lower them, by definition. If everybody pays the same rate, and if that rate raises the same revenue as the current system, then some people must be paying more and others less. Proponents of the flat tax counter that fairness demands equality under the law, while opponents argue that fairness demands a higher rate from greater incomes. But whatever the outcome of the moral argument, the economic argument is dubious. The poor and middle class would lose precisely what the rich would gain. The resulting reduction in the take-home pay of the average worker must have a negative impact on aggregate demand. The rich simply cannot spend or invest their increased incomes fast enough to make up for the losses in wages. This is a phenomenon known as the *velocity of money*. Money simply moves faster (is more efficient) at the lower end of the income scale. For example, if you give a dollar to a poor man, he immediately takes it to lunch, or spends it to fulfill some other pressing need. But if you give the same dollar to Bill Gates, he doesn't know what to do with it. It fills no immediate need and takes a long vacation before it does any work. During that vacation, it represents purchasing power lost to the economy.

But that is not the only problem with this scheme. The two real problems are, that the flat tax radically changes our notions of financial accounting, and that it conflates "exemptions" with "loopholes." To take the latter problem first, an "exemption" is some provision in the tax code that allows a person or firm to deduct some specific expense, such as charitable contributions or mortgage interest, from their income. There are thousands of these exemptions in the tax code, most of which benefit some preferred business group. But while an exemption is something specifically addressed in the tax code, a loophole is just the opposite: it deals with situations that are *not* addressed in the code, but which arise in real business situations and about which the taxpayer is allowed to make his own ruling, a ruling he usually makes in his own favor. There are excellent arguments for eliminating all or most of the exemptions; there are no good arguments for multiplying loopholes. Exemptions are eliminated by *repealing* portions of the tax code, but loopholes are eliminated by *adding* to it. The fair tax proponents want to slim down the sixty-thousand-page tax code to a few pages. But while this will eliminate all the exemptions, it will multiply the loopholes exponentially.

Why? This brings us to the first issue: the treatment of revenue, expenses, and income as simple and uncomplicated notions. But this is not so. If you ask an accountant how to compute a firm's expenses or income, he will point you to the Financial Accounting Standards Board's rulings, which run several volumes, and which are always growing as new situations arise. No tax code that deals with income can be any shorter than the Generally Accepted Accounting Principles (GAAP), and in fact must be some multiple of them, since the accounting standards allow wide latitude in the choice of methods; a latitude that would simply allow businesses to choose their reported income, which would, in effect, abolish any tax on business. Income taxes can only work to the extent that they are intrusive and complex, and any attempt to "simplify" them turns the tax code into a series of loopholes that benefit mostly the rich and shift the entire burden of taxation onto labor.

In fact, the flat tax as it applies to business is really a cash-flow tax rather than an income tax. A business would pay no taxes on its investment income, but interest expense would not be deductible, which sounds bizarre. Equally bizarre is the provision that payments for "fringe" benefits, including the employer-paid Social Security tax and health insurance, would not be deductible. This would force these payments to be made as "wages" and therefore taxable to the employee at the 32.3 percent rate. It is hard to interpret this provision as anything but a direct and gratuitous attack on labor.

The "Fair" Tax

If incomes cannot be taxed without an intrusive and complex code, what about consumption? This is the idea behind the so-called fair tax, which is actually a national sales tax of 30 percent. Unlike the flat tax, this tax would replace all income, Social Security, and Medicare taxes, and would be levied on purchases of new goods and services by all consumers and governments. Business purchases would be exempt. "All" purchases here means just that: cars, homes, medical services, drugs, food, insurance policies, etc.

Since a 30 percent tax would cripple the poor, a monthly "prebate" would be given to all citizens, equal to a "consumption allowance" calculated to be near the poverty line. For example, a single person would have a consumption allowance of $10,400 per year, and 23 percent of that amount would be "prebated" to him on a monthly basis at a rate of $199 per month. A family of four would get a "prebate" of $567 per month. This amount would go to all citizens, whether they were poor or not; everyone would be on the welfare system.

Fair tax proponents believe that the entire Internal Revenue Service and its army of agents could be eliminated because the current state sales-tax agencies would collect the tax. They argue that the accounting expenses of the tax code would be eliminated, prices would go down because there are no tax expenses on production, and that there would be no deductions on paychecks so that workers would keep all that they earn. Further, the proponents claim that there would be no room for fraud. All of these claims can be easily shown to be false or even fraudulent.

The first problem is that fraud would be rampant, and the new system would create many opportunities for fraud. The first opportunity is that all business purchases are exempt. But since the elimination of the income tax means that businesses no longer report their incomes to the government, everybody will want to declare themselves a "business" and exempt all of their purchases. Without auditing their books, it will be impossible to know whether or not they really are a business or just a tax dodge. In order to prevent such fraud, you would have to have a reporting system similar to the one that is already in place. The second opportunity for fraud comes from legitimate businesses converting all of the living expenses of their owners or employees into business expenses, thereby making them exempt from the tax. Without auditing their books, it will be impossible to say if the expense actually is a business or a personal expense. The third source of fraud comes in the exemption for "used" goods. The plan does not define a "new" and "used" good, nor does it define a method to distinguish between the two. The simplest way would be to define a "used" good as something upon which the tax had previously been paid. But this would require an enormous record-keeping system, and the system would be easy to avoid. For example, suppose a builder had a new home valued at $300,000, upon which a tax of $90,000 would have to be paid, for a total price of $390,000. Instead, he "sells" it to a confederate for $100,000 plus the tax, now $30,000. Now he has a "used" home, and can sell it for what he likes with no tax. He sells it for $360,000, pays his confederate a commission, and undersells his competition by $30,000. But the biggest source of fraud would be in false identification papers. Since every citizen is entitled to a "prebate," the traffic in manufactured IDs would be tremendous. No self-respecting crook would be without at least ten Social Security cards, and the "prebate" that goes with them. Short of the establishment of a police state, it would be impossible to monitor all citizens closely enough to see if they were real persons or imaginary ones.

Nor would this proposal eliminate the IRS. On the contrary, it would vastly expand its powers. It is true that most states have a mechanism for collecting sales taxes, but they all operate under different rules. And no state has a sales tax that intrudes into the doctor's office, home sales, insurance payments, and every other possible purchase. All fifty state departments would have to be put under the direct supervision of the IRS. Further, a vast welfare apparatus would have to be created to pay the "prebate," a welfare department that would cover every citizen, whether real or fraudulent. This would constitute the largest expansion of government intrusion into the life of its citizens since the establishment of the income tax itself.

The proponents of the fair tax claim that pretax prices would go down by an amount equal to the tax itself, since businesses would no longer be paying any taxes. But it is not at all clear that this would happen. Certainly, *some* prices would go down, for items made in this country by firms in highly competitive markets. But this is hardly true of all products, or even most of them. For example, it will have no effect on the price of oil; the Arabs will not give us a break because we have an unreasonable sales tax. Indeed, it will have no effect on imports in general, which are, alas, a large part of our consumption. In truth, nobody can know what the effects of such a tax would be, because it would constitute the biggest government intervention into free-market pricing since the Russian Revolution; we simply have no experience to guide us in assessing the effects of such a massive intervention.

One cost that would go up under the fair tax is the cost of state and local government. This is because government purchases are taxed under this plan. And these governments, unlike everybody else, are not likely to engage in tax dodges. Now, at the federal level, this makes little difference; the government both pays and collects the tax; there will merely be some additional bookkeeping costs. But state and local governments will have to raise property and other taxes to pay for the 30 percent increase in the cost of their purchases.

Finally, for people who must consume all or most of what they make, a sales tax is the equivalent of an income tax; all of their income must be converted to purchases. Every dollar earned beyond the poverty rate will be taxed at 30 percent, a rate near what the rich pay on their last dollar earned.

Is Reform Possible?

I could offer further critiques of both of these tax plans, but the more interesting question is why two such obviously flawed—indeed, harebrained—tax schemes could generate such support and loyalty. Part of the reason is ideological. People raised on standard economic theory tend to believe that it is wrong to tax capital in any way; they have been taught that capital is the driver of growth, and taxes on capital limit growth more than any other tax. Hence labor, and labor alone, must bear all the burden of taxation. Whatever the differences in these plans, this is the one point upon which they agree. Now, it is certainly true that a tax on anything limits that thing. Hence, a tax on capital limits capital formation (to what degree, however, is debatable). However, a tax on labor limits labor, and labor, not capital, is the true source of all economic values. To limit labor is to eventually limit capital formation; the two have the same source.

The second reason is that people are genuinely disgusted with the intrusive nature of the income tax and the government bloat that seems to accompany it. All of our financial dealings must be reported to officers of the state, which is sure to make us all uncomfortable, even when we acknowledge the necessity of paying taxes.

The third reason is that people see the tax code as nothing but a network of loopholes, a veritable tunnel system that allows the rich and well-connected to get around any meaningful taxation, and they believe that these systems will somehow change that. Of course, the "reforms" will just make this worse, but it is the perception rather than the reality that counts in politics.

If the flat and fair taxes are not a practical basis for tax reform, are we limited to fiddling with the various rules and rates that make up the current codes? We have seen this kind of "reform" for the last thirty years and especially in the last eight. The results have not been encouraging. Even in the so-called recovery, growth rates were sluggish and seemed to be driven not by any real growth, but by a mere credit bubble in housing, a bubble that has now collapsed with disastrous consequences. Indeed, during this time, the median wage actually fell. And above it all, the debt of the United States is expanding at a dangerous rate. The national debt's interest now comes to half-a-trillion dollars per year and is rising.

If the Republican plan has been a disaster, will a "reform" in the other direction work? Obviously, it will work as well (or as poorly) as it worked in the past. These reforms generally have the effect of broadening the tax base to include more capital income, and redistributing that income. This has the effect of giving a slight preference to labor, or it would if all the odd exemptions were eliminated.

All of these debates center around the question of whether capital or labor should get preferential treatment. But is this really a rational question? On the one hand, it seems bizarre to tax the labor of a man who digs ditches for a living, while exempting the labor of another who only clips coupons. On the other hand, if the bonds that the coupon-clipper clips represent savings from his past labor, his prior-period ditch-digging, why should he be penalized in any way? So the real question is, "Should labor and capital be taxed at all, or, if they are, should they be the primary source of government revenue?"

From our current perspective, this question is astounding. Income taxes are the mainstay of the federal budget, most state budgets, and even many city budgets. Could these taxes be abolished or significantly reduced without wrecking all public finances? What could possibly replace them? Income taxes, however, are not a constant in human history, nor even in American history. The founders recognized the possibility of an income tax and prohibited it in the Constitution. It was not until the Sixteenth Amendment was passed in 1913 that the tax had a legal basis. The tax was originally 7 percent of incomes over $500,000, an enormous sum in those days that would likely have affected a few hundred persons at most. Therefore, the income tax was really a tax on concentrated wealth. But under the pressure of war, debt, and depressions, the rates went up and the minimum income level went down, so that it quickly became a labor tax.

Historically, such taxes have always been regarded as suspicious, or even a sign of oppression. In 1381, for example, when Richard II imposed a poll tax (essentially, a labor tax), the result was Wat Tyler's rebellion, which gathered widespread support across England and quickly captured London and the king. Tyler nearly succeeded in establishing a republican form of government in England centuries before it actually happened, and would have done so, had not Richard reneged on the promises he was forced to sign and had Tyler killed after his army disbanded. Would that we were as conscious of our rights as were the medieval peasants.

But if we exclude or severely limit these taxes, what is left? An age that requires battleships for defense and freeways for transportation might be somewhat more expensive to run than fourteenth-century England. How will we finance such things? That question can only be answered if we first answer questions about the scale and scope of government, and the government's role in producing the wealth and prosperity that we all share, or wish to share. These questions are the subject of the next chapter.

13

The Proper Role of Government

What Should the Government Be Doing?

Milton Friedman famously remarked that if the government were put in charge of the Sahara, there would soon be a shortage of sand. It is a remark that delighted both libertarian and neoclassical economists. It is likely that Friedman repeated this remark at many a seminar. To do so, he had to leave his home, one built according to strict building codes and protected by the socialized services of the city police and fire departments, travel over socialized roads and freeways to a government-sponsored and government-regulated airport, board an airplane after it had been thoroughly vetted by a government-supervised inspector, all before he even got to the seminar. And all of this took place under the protection of a military establishment which involves considerable expense to the government and its citizens.

It would seem, then, that the government does indeed do many things tolerably well. It may be, as Friedman claimed, that most of these services could be provided by the private market. And while that might be true, and in some cases must be true, it is equally true that while many egregious examples of inefficiency can be found, the government provides many services tolerably well and with as much efficiency as can be found in any large bureaucracy, public or private. Nevertheless, the point of Friedman's remark is still valid: what should government be doing, and at what level should it be doing it? While conservatives leave little room for government and socialists leave little room for anything else, neither provides us with a set of principles by which we can evaluate the proper role of government.

Man is a social animal; he needs government. We are born into the little ready-made communities called "families" ruled in various ways by parents. We organize ourselves into social and political hierarchies as naturally as we breathe, and we need government to help fulfill our natural ends and goals. But while government in theory may be natural, any actual government may not fulfill the natural ends and goals of man—and most don't. The modern nation-state becomes an end in itself, and the citizen a mere client and, often, an actual servant. We need some set of principles by which to distinguish good government from bad, and the all-or-nothing arguments of socialists and conservatives are not helpful. Until we decide on the proper role of government, we cannot possibly talk about the proper level and kind of taxation that is required to support the government.

Associated with the question of what the government should be doing is the question of at what level the government should be doing it. During the 2008 presidential election campaign, Senator Joe Biden boasted that he had sponsored legislation which had placed eleven thousand cops on the beat in our cities. But while his boast is likely true, it is somewhat frightening when a problem that we would normally take to our local mayor and city council is resolved at the highest level of government. Every local problem becomes a federal case, and the level of government farthest from the actual situation becomes the guarantor of the cop on the beat, the teacher in the classroom, and every other aspect of our social lives that is normally resolved by local action.

"Starving the Beast"

The question of the proper role and level of government has become a difficult one because each new government expenditure creates a constituency ready to fight for the expansion of the role of government and especially for the expansion of their particular subsidy. Thus, addressing the question at a practical level involves battling a thousand constituencies, each with a hundred lobbyists and millions of dollars in campaign contributions or promises of lucrative jobs. These special interests easily combine to defeat any serious attempt at budget and government reform.

Recognizing this problem, the Reagan administration abandoned the question of the proper role of government and opted for a strategy of "starving the beast," that is, cutting taxes and thereby cutting off the air supply to big government. The resulting superdeficits would force a confrontation over the issue of government spending. Alas, the strategy did not work. The beast's diet was merely changed from cash to credit, and it turns out that credit is easier to spend than cash. The government did not shrink, but grew, and grew at an alarming rate. The budget deficit tripled under Reagan-Bush (from $700 million to $2.1 trillion), more than doubled again under Clinton (to over $5 trillion), and more than doubled again under George W. Bush (to nearly $11 trillion). What is really troublesome about the deficit, however, is not the absolute number itself, but the size of the interest payments, which, as of this writing, amount to about half-a-trillion dollars each year. This works out to about $1,500 per person, or $6,000 for a family of four. This means that the first $6,000 of each family's taxes goes to financing the past, with nothing for the present or the future. Sooner or later, the past must overwhelm the present and foreclose the future. Then the beast will indeed starve, but so will the rest of us. Financing the present by mortgaging the future is not only bad economics, it is bad morals; we pay for our profligacy by burdening our children, thereby reversing the natural order of family and national life.

But the Reagan administration had another reason for their "starve the beast" strategy: they really had no philosophy of governance. They only knew that they wanted "less government," but they were not quite clear on what that meant in practice. By and large, they were followers of Friedrich Hayek, the Austrian economist. The Austrian economists limit the role of government to "protecting property," but they are vague as to what that actually means. Indeed, they are vague about what "property" means, since this is a term that has had many definitions over the course of the centuries. Nor could they give clear reasons why this should be the only function of government; after all, if everything is to be privatized, why not privatize this function as well, and leave property to those who can protect it with their own resources? Hayek himself equivocated on the issue of government, allowing that it could provide basic incomes and health care, handle externalities of the market, and other functions as well. In the end, Hayek ended up refusing the question of the proper role of government and hence could give no clear guidance to his acolytes in the Reagan administration. In practice, Austrian economics proved to be a faster road to socialism than the socialists themselves could build, but it was mainly a socialism for the rich. Since it is a woefully incomplete theory, its unintended consequences overwhelm its theoretical bases with the result that Austrian theory leads to socialist practice, which is exactly the result that Hilaire Belloc predicted for such theories in his book, *The Servile State*.

Until we answer the question about government, we cannot answer the question about taxes; unless we know what the government ought to do, we cannot know how much it ought to cost or how to fund it. And we cannot know what it ought to do without first knowing what purpose government has and upon what principles it rests.

The Purpose of Government

Human beings are not self-sufficient as individuals. We are born naked against the elements and helpless in ourselves; we are dependent upon others from the beginning, and apart from them we would not last our first day on earth. This dependency continues throughout our lives, since none of us can or should acquire all the skills necessary to grow our own food, make our own shoes, provide our own education, etc. We are by nature social beings and thrive only in community. Therefore, *the purpose of government is to provide the conditions under which all the other communities that make up the social fabric can flourish.* First and foremost among these other communities is the community of the family, the one that first calls us into being through an act of love and gives us the gifts that will form us—not only the material gifts of food, clothing, and shelter, but also the gifts of language, of culture, of our first experience of love and belonging, and, most importantly, the gift of a *name,* a name that ties us to family but is uniquely ours, the name that lets us know that we are both part of something and unique beings.

At once we note that we are at odds with the modern political and economic theories, which are built on the *individual* as the prime social and economic unit. But this is not correct because the individual, apart from the social order, is not capable of providing for himself. Indeed, the individual is not even capable of reproducing himself. The individual flourishes in and through the community. This is not to denigrate the value of the individual person, since the purpose of the family is to allow the person to flourish; it is to note that persons only exist in and through communities, first and foremost the community of the family.

Therefore, we can judge the success or failure of government by noting the strength of the family units that make up the society. If they are barely surviving and chronically in debt, if mothers are forced to work by economic conditions and unable to attend to the education of their children, if families seem to be temporary and chronically subject to dissolution, if the children have only limited educational opportunities, if they are only concerned with the getting (and destruction) of more *things* for their happiness, then we may say that the family is materially, morally, and spiritually weak. Alas, these are the conditions that describe too many American families today, and the failure of the family leads to failures in the economic, political, and social orders, failures which have no solution apart from repairing our damaged families.

Starting with the family, we can go on to assess the health of larger communities, not only governmental ones like cities and states, but those communities of work and social life in which we find ourselves and through which we contribute to the common good and to our own development.

In order to flourish, all of these communities require certain things. They require a material base by way of access to productive property which they can own or share; they require training and education; they require relatively free markets; they require a culture of liberty in which they can grow; they require a certain set of shared values if they are to share a common cultural space; they require certain infrastructures such as roads, a money system, and courts. Some of these things are or can be directly supplied by the government and others are merely influenced by its decisions. But all the decisions of government must be based on a recognition of their effect on these communities. Government is not, of course, solely responsible for the flourishing of these communities (that would be socialism or paternalism), but it is often responsible for their failure. In order to assure that the government is acting on behalf of these communities, there are certain bedrock principles that must be followed, no matter what the form of government.

The Principles of Government

It seems today as if government is no more than a competition among special interests, each fighting for a share of the public purse and a list of privileges from public law. Along with this we note a centralizing tendency that transcends party rhetoric and leads to an ever-growing central government, which displaces all lower units of government and even private association. Of course, such competition for power must favor the powerful. This self-aggrandizing tendency of government mirrors a similar cult of bigness in the commercial realm. Companies grow "too big to fail," and hence can act with impunity, knowing that no matter how foolish their actions, they can always have recourse to the public purse; they can rely on economic blackmail: "If we fail, everything fails; bail us or be damned!" As I write this, the government is committing trillions of dollars to private bailouts, a perfect socialism for the rich necessary to save everybody else. But this is not the first time this has happened; indeed, it is a chronic condition of corporate capitalism. There have been about nineteen bailouts in the last one hundred years, making them fairly predictable events. The bailouts get bigger as the corporations and the government grow in size.

Yet bailouts have never reached the size and scale of today's crisis, and it is likely that the system will not work and must be reformed, probably after a complete collapse. A reform of the system will require an understanding of the proper principles of government. And these principles are the exact opposite of the practice of modern government. Against the clash of special interests, we assert "The Principle of The Common Good"; against the centralizing tendency, we assert "The Principle of Subsidiarity"; against the tendency to favor the rich and powerful, we assert "The Principle of Solidarity."

The Common Good

The idea of the common good would seem self-evident, but in fact most modern political and economic thought is based on the priority of private and personal goods. "Greed is good" has become an implicit assumption of our political and economic lives. This idea was first advanced in 1714 in Bernard de Mandeville's *The Fable of the Bees,* which was subtitled *Private Vices, Publick Benefits.* Mandeville offered the paradox that private vice was the key to public virtue, that the water of private interest could be transformed into the wine of the common good. But this view is far too mystical. It is based on the idea that the common good is no more than a summation of individual and particular goods, and that there is no transcendent good which unites us all.

But clearly, this is not true. The individual good of a father, for example, could run counter to the good of his family. The father who spends the bulk of his earnings on himself and his own pleasures and leaves little for the feeding of his family and nothing for the education of his children indulges a private good at the expense of the common good of the family. It is only by realizing himself in and through the family that his good and the good of the family can be united. And this is the key to realizing the common good: we must develop the sense that our particular goods are bound up with the common good. We cannot truly be successful at the expense of our neighbors; their success and ours are connected.

The great difficulty of recognizing the common good is that we are all members of the community mostly through participation in particular communities, each of which makes a partial contribution to the common good. That is, we participate in the overall community in and through our participation in, say, the arts community, the business community, the educational community, etc. The end of each of these communities is partial and *private,* in the sense of the Latin term, *privatus,* which connotes a lack of something, a privation. The tendency of private communities is to let their partial and private ends dominate the contribution they make to the public and general good. But the common good cannot flourish unless we recognize that our particular communities depend on, and are ultimately successful through, the success of the whole community. This takes a constant recognition of the wider community and a constant effort of the will to limit our demands on the community only to what is necessary for, and proportional to, our contributions to that wider community.

Subsidiarity

As members of vast, modern nation-states, especially those governed by the principles of pure individualism, we cannot help but see ourselves as mere infinitesimal cogs in a vast machine over which we have very little control, save for annual, semiannual, or quadrennial plebiscites in which we get to choose leaders from a very limited list. Indeed, due to the miracle of national television, the government official most remote from us, the president, is a daily presence in our living room, while the person who might be our neighbor, the local mayor or city councilman, remains a stranger whose very name we cannot recall. In other words, we have stood the natural order of government and social life on its head, with the most remote becoming more important than the local.

In opposition to this centralizing tendency, solidarity implies a "bottom-up" view of society. It starts with the family as the basic unit of society. All economic, social, and political activity is built around the family and serves its needs. But because no family is self-sufficient, it requires economic and social contexts, including government. Higher social formations have a right to interfere in the affairs of lower organizations, including the family, but this is only a limited right; such interventions can only be used to correct egregious failures, and may last only for as long as necessary to correct the failure. Some problems, of course, don't go away, such as unemployment. As long as the economic system is unable to offer all persons meaningful employment, then society must provide other means for their dignified subsistence. But this must be clearly seen as a defect of the system, in the same way that the need for a police force or an army is really a defect arising from original sin. From the viewpoint of subsidiarity, society is highly "textured"; instead of a simple system of an individual-to-government relationship, there should be a rich collection of levels within society, each with its own realm of competence and authority. At present, government has absorbed functions which used to belong to the church or other authorities such as the guilds. Marriage, education, charity, and commercial regulations had been guided by other bodies, even if their decisions were enforced by the state. The all-powerful, centralized state has displaced all of these other and (I contend) more natural authorities. Other authorities, even the family itself, exist only by the sufferance of the central administration.

According to the principle of subsidiarity, the higher-level organization can only justify its existence by the necessary support it gives to lower-level ones. Assuming that most functions of political, social, and economic life can be adequately handled at the local level, the higher levels are therefore the least important, and their importance diminishes the higher up they are. This does not mean that they have no meaning-ful authority, nor any right to intervene. For example, we know that African Americans would not enjoy full citizenship in America were it not for forceful interventions by the central government. But even this intervention is instructive, since it involves a community that extends beyond any local jurisdiction, and was clearly oppressed in many (even all) jurisdictions at least to some degree. And since the oppression was egregious, it was clearly the right and duty of the central government to act, even in disregard of local rights. Nevertheless, such interventions should be made only on clear necessity, only as much as necessary, and only for as long as necessary. In general, local organizations should be free to develop in their own way and with their own resources.

One important point that needs to be made about subsidiarity is that not only should *control* be as local as possible, but *funding* should be as well. If the funding for governmental programs comes from afar without directly impacting local resources, it appears to be "free" money, which always distorts the decision-making process. If someone else pays, we can never have enough; when the money comes from our own resources, we tend to spend it as conservatively as we can. This does not preclude higher authorities from making contributions to local programs, but such contributions must be related to the com-mon good; it does the local authority no good to become dependent on the remote power. This is, as we shall see, one of the most important principles in government funding and taxation.

Solidarity

Solidarity is complementary with subsidiarity. Subsidiarity provides the vertical dimension of life, while solidarity provides the horizon-tal dimension; subsidiarity is a connection between elements of society viewed as a hierarchy, while solidarity provides the connections between the elements viewed as if they were on the same level. Solidarity connects us with the common good and impels us, in the name of Christian charity, to act for the good of all. There can be no vision of the common good unless there is solidarity among all the elements of society.

Of particular importance to solidarity is *the preferential option for the poor*. When we act in solidarity, we act for the good of all. The preferential option for the poor serves as a practical test of whether we are acting for all, or just for some. Under the preferential option, we always examine the effects of any action on the poorest of our neighbors; if it is not good for them, it breaks solidarity. Since we are all inclined to opportunism and rationalization, solidarity, particularly when it forces us to look at our actions from the standpoint of the poor, helps ensure the common good.

If what we have said so far is correct, then we have provided a purpose for government and the principles of government, and with these tools we can examine our actually existing government to see how well it conforms to purpose and principle, and ask what can be done to change it.

14

The Cost of Government

So What's Wrong with Big Government?

Taxes at all levels of government currently consume about $5 trillion out of a $14 trillion economy, or more than a third of the Gross Domestic Product. The federal budget alone consumes about 20 percent of the GDP. There are of course great debates about the effects of such large expenditures. Some see it as a drag on the economy; government expenditures, they say, crowd out private investment and thereby slow the economy. If the economy were running at anywhere near full employment of labor and capital, this would be true. But this has seldom been the case; in general, capitalism has proven unable, historically, to maintain full employment for any appreciable length of time. Hence, government expenditures, instead of crowding out investment or demand, have been a significant source of both.

Moreover, the history of American capitalism bears this out. In the period before the Great Depression, the federal budget generally ran 3–5 percent of the GDP. Since the Second World War, it has run 18–23 percent. Yet, the economy has been far more stable in this latter period (see chapter 2). So the question is, "Do we really *want* to cut the budget?" Indeed, we can ask whether capitalism is capable of functioning without such gargantuan government. "Big" capitalism seems to require big government for its proper functioning. But the distributist seeks to do away with both, or at least significantly modify them. And from the distributist perspective, there are at least five problems with such gargantuan government:

1. It encourages political centralization. Governance migrates to the level with the greatest taxing authority, which is the central government. The central authority displaces local government. Thus it is that a senator can boast of putting "cops on the beat," acting in place of a mayor or town councilman.

2. It encourages gigantism in business in two ways. The first is that the regulatory requirements are a great burden for small businesses, but form only a small part of the overhead for large businesses. As the central authority grows, its reporting and regulatory apparatus grows, and this becomes a great barrier to the formation of small businesses, who often have the same requirements as the corporate giants. Small businesses must devote a proportionally larger share of their resources to meeting regulations, and arc thus at a disadvantage to large businesses. This becomes a great and often insurmountable obstacle to entrepreneurship. The second way that huge government promotes gigantism in business is that large entities are better at obtaining contracts, subsidies, tax exemptions, and privileges from the government. Their very size and scale make them more politically powerful, because they can devote more resources to political and lobbying activities. This converts democracy into an oligarchy of special interests.

3. Governments tend to misallocate resources by reducing their

costs, often to zero. Some things should, of course, be treated as common resources, freely available to all who can make use of them. Education, for example, surely falls in that category. But other things are economic resources that should be allocated either purely or mainly by economic means. Such things as *free*ways and free levees, for example, distort economic incentives and become subsidies that distort the free markets, and favor some groups over others.

4. Such a highly government-dependent economy is not sustainable. As the economy becomes more and more dependent on government stimuli, each round must be greater than the last to have even a marginal effect. Eventually, the cost of stimuli must exceed the effects, and the whole system collapses of its own weight. Hence, while the Keynesian system has worked, more or less, for the last sixty years, it may have passed its sell-by date. Indeed, the current crisis of a more-or-less Keynesian economic system might be its last.

5. But the worst effect is that a giant government increases *servility* and *dependence*. More and more, we cease to be real *citizens* and become mere clients of the state, mere employees of the corporation. Our lives are suffocated between these two great powers. Our relationship to the governing authorities (which includes the corporations) becomes a matter of giving as little as we can get away with while demanding as much as we can get. Notions of the common good—notions that are associated with true citizenship—disappear and our political and economic lives are lived entirely at the level of self-interest, a level which can never sustain a community or a nation.

The first four of these problems are violations of solidarity and subsidiarity, and the fifth is a natural result of violating these principles. That is to say, we can have justice in our political and economic lives, or we can have servility, and we have to make a conscious choice. Our choices in this matter are most concretely expressed in government by the size and scope of their budgets, by what we choose to fund and how we choose to fund it. And when expenditures reach the level they have, it is inevitable that the government must reach into every aspect of our lives.

The answers to the current crisis involve spending more and spending it from the top, from Washington and other capitals all over the world. Within the logic of the world economic system for the last sixty years, this makes a lot of sense; it is the "right thing" to do. But at some point, this "right thing" becomes the wrong thing. We have bailed out enterprises because they claim that they are "too big to fail," but the distributist knows instinctively that they are too big to succeed, at least without government support. The proper response is to break them up into more manageable and more numerous enterprises, any one of which may fail without bringing down the whole system. But this also means that we must attack the basis of their power, which is the centralization of government and the huge revenue base that goes with it and forms such a tempting target.

If we wish to transition from a Keynesian capitalism to a political economy of distributed ownership, we must first reduce the federal budget and the power that goes with it. That is, economic distributism requires a political distributism; power must be redistributed to the lower levels of government and the centralizing (and socialistic) tendencies must be overcome.

Can We Cut the Budget?

The major strategy for cutting the budget since Ronald Reagan has been a "starve the beast" approach, whereby taxes are cut and the resulting fiscal crisis is supposed to force cuts in spending. But clearly this strategy has been counterproductive. It is not really tax-cutting at all, just tax-shifting. The government grows in size and scope, but the costs are shifted to the next generation. This is both immoral and unwise. It is of course immoral to charge our children for services we consume. And indeed, it is only possible because foreign governments have decided to finance our profligacy, an act which guarantees a market for their own goods and gives them increasing influence in American affairs.

The federal budget process itself has been an exercise in despair, for two reasons: first, because most of the expenses are labeled "mandatory," Congress can only nibble at the edges; likewise, whatever the labels, every line item has a lobby all its own, lobbies which combine to kill any real reform. It can only be by a concerted effort of political will that the budget can be cut and the power returned once again to the regions, states, and cities. Political will is not available in the present economic system, because the system itself has been socialized and made dependent on these expenditures. Thus the problem is that we cannot change the economic system until we decide to change the budget, and we cannot change the budget until we decide to change the economic system.

Distributism is the key to this whole process, because it gives us a proven system to work toward and a way to cut the budget. I believe that by using distributist principles, the federal burden can easily be cut by a third to a half over the course of ten years. Moreover, *it can be cut without impacting any essential services* now provided by the government. This is rather a large claim, and it is therefore necessary to demonstrate exactly what I mean, and how distributism helps cut the expense of government.

Cutting the Budget

The 2007 federal budget came to about $2.86 trillion, a substantial number. To show how it can be seriously reduced, I will address just a few items in the budget. I offer the caveat that the budget is a highly technical work of art, and I do not claim any great skill as a budget analyst.

National Defense

National defense is an intrinsic function of any government; the world being what it is, if the nation cannot be defended it cannot long endure. This function cost the United States $626 billion in 2007, or about 22 percent of the entire budget. Indeed, the United States spends almost as much as the rest of the world combined. The actual cost is much higher, because two wars have depleted military equipment that must be replaced, and left a large number of wounded who must be cared for. But for all of this money, America has a rather small standing army (although a rather large navy and air force)—about forty-two brigades—that has found it difficult to sustain even small wars without repeated deployments. It would be a mistake, however, to believe that the national defense budget is all about national defense. It is also about international hegemony—the ability to force our will on the world—and about economic subsidies.

Hegemony turns out to be illusive and expensive, if not downright counterproductive; far from enforcing our will on the world, our presence so far from home is often the source of opposition to American policy. The United States has between seven hundred and one thousand bases and installations around the world (the exact number is a state secret). The American military is the mainstay of European and Far East defense. This certainly made sense in the years following World

War II, when the world was in ruins and the Soviet Union was in an expansive mood. However, Europe and Japan are now rich places, capable of providing for their own defense; it is no longer necessary for them to outsource the job to America, and no longer in our best interest to perform this task. The result is that Americans are taxed to subsidize the defense of our economic competitors. They spend less of their resources in building their own defense and more in building their industries.

But the national defense also serves as an ongoing economic stimulus package, one with enormous consequences. This is the "military-industrial complex" that President Eisenhower warned about in his farewell address. Procurement and research consumed $211 billion of the budget. Often, these are for weapons which the military neither needs nor wants, but are important to lobbyists and politicians. Naturally, we constantly need to replace and upgrade military equipment, but these budgets are so large that they cannot easily be monitored or controlled, and stand as an open invitation to corruption. Indeed, high ranking officers routinely retire to lucrative jobs and directorships with defense contractors, a system that cannot avoid the appearance of payoffs and institutionalized bribery.

By recalling our army to our shores and investing only in what is needed for a modern army, I believe that we could easily cut a third of the budget while strengthening our real defense. Distributists know instinctively that our best defense lies closest to home, and that billions spent around the world does more to strengthen our enemies and subsidize our competitors. This would save $208 billion and improve our defenses.

International Affairs

There is $31 billion in the U.S. federal budget for international aid and military assistance. This "aid" often goes to prop up military dictatorships and to fund corruption on an international scale. It is not that we who are wealthy should be reluctant to aid those who are poor. Indeed, this is even to our own natural advantage. But all the evidence points toward aid retarding development rather than aiding it. This will be dealt with more fully in the chapter on globalization and development, but for now, I believe that we can cut $15 billion and actually be more effective.

Natural Resources

Nearly $34 billion of the budget is labeled "natural resources," and its major purpose seems to be to turn natural resources into unnatural ones. The Mississippi, for example, is no longer a river but the world's greatest drainage ditch, hemmed in by walls forty feet or higher along its entire length. This is called "flood control," but in fact it prevents the river from being a river, because one thing that rivers ought to do is flood. It makes sense to protect great cities from these floods, but that task is made more difficult—and less certain—by trying to keep the whole river from ever flooding anything. Floods improve the natural fertility of the soil by adding new deposits of mud and silt. But since the levees are "free" to everyone who wants them, everybody wants them. The costs of levees should be borne primarily by the land made safe by the levee. This is not to say that there should not be some contribution at the national level; the entire nation benefits from the Mississippi. Nevertheless, the control of this river—or any river—should be primarily the responsibility of the communities that border that river.

When those who bear the costs make the decisions, they are likely to make better decisions. For example, the lower Ninth Ward in New Orleans flooded after Hurricane Katrina. But in fact, the ward is part of the natural floodplain, and would never have been developed—at least not in the way it was—if the developers had been required to bear the costs of the levees. And this is the story all over. People build their homes in places prone to fire, flood, hurricane, and earthquake, but take no account of these dangers because someone else bears the cost. Natural systems are perverted into unnatural ones, and natural development is made unnatural by federal subsidies. We could do more for natural resources by spending less, by being unwilling to carry on a war against nature and a program of subsidies. This budget can be cut by $15 billion, and the natural systems strengthened in the process.

Agriculture

America is believed to have the most efficient agriculture in the world, but if we judge the matter by the number of subsidies it claims to require, we would have to conclude that it is the least efficient system. The agriculture budget is $23 billion, of which $14 billion is labeled "farm income stabilization." Now, farming is a hazardous business, one subject to the vicissitudes not only of the market, but of the weather as well. The original idea of these farm programs was to stabilize the "family farm," but the actual effect has been to replace the family farm with agribusiness. It would consume volumes to detail what is wrong with these programs, but let me first concede that it is important to have crop insurance and similar programs. However, these programs should be primarily supported by the farmers, by the farming states, and by those businesses that have a direct interest in farms, such as feed, fertilizer, and equipment suppliers. Like any other business, a portion of the profits from the good times should be set aside to cover losses in the bad times. It is the farmers themselves who ought to contribute—and control—farm support programs. They are the best ones to judge how much is needed, and when to disperse the funds. The federal budget should have some support for the farmer, since the nation has a direct interest in a stable food supply, but we certainly don't need to be subsidizing tobacco, sugar, and vast oceans of corn syrup. Therefore, the bulk of the funds should come from and be controlled by farmers, who know their own business best of all. It is not unreasonable, therefore, to cut $10 billion from this budget.

Transportation

The transportation budget runs $79 billion. Yet if we follow the sensible principle that costs should always be allocated, insofar as possible, to those who use the services, no budget should be as easy to cut. In a glaring misnomer, our "freeway" system certainly is not free. In fact, our road system has an enormous cost. And since the roads are subsidized, the cost is not being paid, but is being allowed to accumulate for the next generation. That is to say, roads are physical things which deteriorate and have to be rebuilt periodically. They accrue depreciation, in accounting terms. But this depreciation is not being collected. Indeed, very little is collected from a *free*way.

This very freedom distorts the economy. It is really a system of subsidies from the inner city to the suburbs, from populous regions to empty ones, and from future generations to the current ones. Indeed, there are whole industries, such as "big-box" stores like Wal-Mart, whose whole existence is dependent on these subsidies. The very shape of our cities is determined by these subsidies. People move from the inner cities and buy larger homes than they could otherwise afford on cheaper land in remote areas. Initially, they reach these homes over two-lane, blacktop backroads, but as the population builds and the roads clog, they demand that the government give them a road. And not just any road, but a superhighway. Given their growing political strength, they usually get all that they demand. The effect is that the inner core of cities subsidizes the outer core and the remote suburb; people are taxed to support the suburbanization, to support homes that compete with theirs. Cities pay for their own destruction.

The freeways should be replaced by tolls roads, roads capable of collecting their building, maintenance, operational, and replacement costs. At one time there was a good argument against doing this because the cost of collecting the tolls was very high and caused great bottlenecks in traffic. However, in this day of Radio-Frequency Identification (RFID) devices, "toll tags" that automatically measure usage, this argument disappears. What is true of the freeways is true of nearly all the transportation subsidies. This is the easiest system to charge back to the actual users. By financing in this way, we could easily cut $40 billion from the budget, while ensuring that there are always sufficient funds both for road building and replacement.

Education

The Department of Education has a $94 billion budget, and yet the whole department should be abolished. There are fifty departments of education, and the federal government adds nothing to the conversation except another level of bureaucracy. There are, no doubt, states that underperform, states that fail their children. But the very existence of fifty systems means that there is always something against which we can compare various approaches. It is possible that federalizing education will stardardize success, but it is also possible, and much more likely, that it will federalize failure.

Interest on the Federal Debt

One often hears complaints about the government "printing" money, but the truth is that almost all of our money is created not by the government but by the banks as "credits" which they create out of thin air. We dealt with this problem in chapter 7, but here I will merely reiterate that it makes no sense to "borrow" the money the banks have created when the public power can simply create that money itself, without interest. Currently, the interest on the federal debt is $430 billion, a number that will rise rapidly due to the bailouts and stimulus.

No real progress can be made if this debt is not eliminated, or at least substantially reduced. In thinking about the debt, one has to think about money itself. In chapter 7 we noted that the creation of money is the private monopoly of the banks. This money is created out of thin air, and represents no prior savings or production. Yet, it forms a claim against things that have been produced. In the case of government debt, the banks lend money they invent, but demand payment in the equivalent of real goods and services. Hence, the government must tax real goods and services and turn over the money to the creditors. But this will become increasingly less of a possibility in the near future.

About 41 percent of the debt ($4.3 trillion) is owned by agencies of the government, mainly the Social Security Trust Fund. This portion of the debt can simply be monetized over a ten- to fifteen-year period, that is, the government will print the money to pay off the debt to the trust funds. Some may be shocked by the suggestion that the government be allowed simply to print money into being, but this is certainly preferable to having the banks lend it into being. Will it be inflationary? It might be mildly so, but if done over ten to fifteen years, it will be no more than simply converting the current interest payments into principle and eliminating both.

There isn't much else that you can do with this debt. The only alternatives (other than just reneging on the commitment) are to raise taxes or increase borrowing. Up until now, Social Security taxes have formed a vast subsidy to the general fund, with IOUs being placed in the fund. But in just a few years, the cash flow will go the other way from the general to the trust funds; but the general fund does not have, and will not have, enough money to pay the trust fund. In order to pay off these IOUs, there would have to be a vast tax increase over and above the high Social Security taxes we now pay. Our children—and the economy—simply cannot tolerate that burden. Or we can simply borrow more money, but that is problematic, to say the least.

The next portion is the 29 percent owed to foreign governments, banks, and individuals. This portion of the debt could be monetized, but likely shouldn't be. My belief is that paying this debt should be the responsibility of the financial sector. A small tax, about 0.25 percent, on the transfer of financial instruments such as stocks, bonds, CDOs, and CDSs. should be levied and placed in a sinking fund to pay the interest and principle on these debts. Such a small tax would be sufficient to pay off the foreign debt over a term of five to ten years.

That leaves only the 31 percent of the debt held by American citizens and institutions. This portion of the debt could be partially monetized (as financial conditions dictate), partially paid off by the sinking fund, or simply left in place and allowed to shrink as a proportion of the economy. *What is critical, however, is that the debt not be allowed to grow.* And this requires abolishing the Fractional Reserve System, whereby the banks get to create money for nothing (as we described in chapter 7). This is the fiat money that is "lent" to the treasury. Its origin is thin air and a legal monopoly, a monopoly that must be abolished.

We cannot continue to live on borrowed money. Even if there is moderate inflation, the debt must be liquidated, and the power to create money must be taken from the banks and returned to the people. And this is not just true for the federal government. Indeed, the Feds should serve as low-interest bankers to the states, funding improvements to the infrastructure and educational systems. Since the money will go to productive purposes, it is not likely to be inflationary, and if it is, we know how to control it (issue less money) and who to blame. The present decrepit method of using the Federal Reserve System to control the money supply not only doesn't work very well, it also imposes huge costs on the economy, tends to manufacture money for purely speculative bubbles, and exists outside the government and hence beyond democratic control.

Subsidiarity in Government Finance

So far, we have identified $812 billion in cuts to the federal budget, or 28 percent, without even touching some of the major areas, such as the welfare system, health care, "community development," research, and the Social Security system. All of these will require major reforms in the near future as they cannot be sustained in their current forms. I am convinced that we can cut at least 50 percent of the federal budget and at the same time actually improve services. The major principle of doing this is always the same: subsidiarity. Expenditures—and the power that goes with them—are relocated to the smallest practical unit of the community. International political ambitions are replaced by real home defense. Costs are, where practical, charged to those who cause the costs.

At this point, however, some critics might note that some of these "cuts" are not cuts at all; they merely relocate expenses to other agencies, such as transportation authorities, levee districts, state budgets, and the like. This critique is absolutely correct. It is not my contention that any of these expenses are not legitimate community functions. Rather, the issue is where to handle these functions, and that will always be at the lowest practical level. Economic distributism requires political distributism, the existence of a diverse set of public powers spread throughout the community. And "power" in this context means the ability to fund things, things like roads and schools and whatever else adds to the common good.

But while political distributism requires that power be dispersed, the dispersal of power itself is dependent on economic distributism. Without reforming the economic system, it will be impossible to reform the political system. The capitalist economy has long been addicted to having a customer and employer as large and as stable as big government, and it is likely that it would collapse without this reliable customer. Before the current era of big government, beginning roughly in the 1940s, the economy was in recession 40 percent of the time. Capitalism requires socialism for its very stability. Those of us who reject socialism find that we must also reject capitalism, because the two go together. Therefore, the capitalist system ought to be replaced by a true "free market" system, and that system is distributism, or something very much like it.

Power in government will always follow the funding source. Whatever level of government has the greatest revenue power will also have the greatest political power. When the federal government acquired the right to tax incomes, it became the greatest source of revenue and hence eclipsed all other sources of authority in the social and political orders. Therefore, it is not only necessary to cut the budget, but also to relocate the taxing authority. If the requirements of the federal government are only half what they are today, we do not need the current oppressive and intrusive tax structure that we have today. Moreover, if we are truly to distribute power to the lower levels of government, then these levels must be the primary taxing authorities, with the federal government having only a residual authority. With this in mind, we can now return to the subject of tax reform.

15

Taxes, Economic Rent, and Externalities

What Should We Tax?

We began our examination of government by looking first at proposals to reform the tax system and noting their deficiencies. We then looked at both the purpose and cost of government and noted that government has exceeded its legitimate purposes and hence its reasonable costs. We can now return to the question of tax reform, and determine how this should be done, because at the heart of governmental reform is tax reform. It is evident by now that the "starve the beast" strategy was a failure; under this strange diet, government "bulked-up" rather than "slimmed-down." Only by identifying the *proper* sources of public revenue, and insisting that government stay within these limits, can we hope to achieve any real reform. So the central question is, "What should we tax?"

There is a bromide about taxes that goes, "If you want less of something, tax it." Currently, the burden of taxation falls on capital and labor. Now, I can't think of any reason why we would want less labor or less capital; therefore, the fairest and best tax on labor and capital is a flat tax of 0 percent, with some notable exceptions, discussed below. But if we eliminate taxes on labor and capital, is there anything left? Is there anything in the economic universe that we want less of? I believe there is. In fact there are two things that can be taxed, one with no impact on economic development, and the other with the deliberate goal of limiting adverse impacts. The first thing is *economic rent* and the second is a tax on *externalities.*

Ground Rent

I repeat here our discussion of economic rent from chapter 10: Economic rent is an amount paid to a factor of production that is more than necessary to keep that factor in production in its current use. It is the very essence of economic inefficiency. For example, the price of steel must be enough to pay for the raw materials in the steel and to compensate the labor and capital that went into making it. If, however, the price rises very much above this amount, then steel claims an economic rent. This rent acts like a tax on all users of the steel, a tax that really doesn't buy anything, but only transfers money from one group (the consumers) to another (the owners). In the case of elastic, reproducible commodities (like steel), this is only a short-term problem, since (in competitive markets) the higher prices attract more labor and capital, the supply is increased, the prices fall, and the economic rent disappears. In the short-term, and for normal commodities, economic rent serves a purpose.

But this does not happen in the case of land; there, the rent is chronic and distorts the returns to both capital and labor. Recall the discussion of the law of ground rents from chapter 9. Ground rent has the first claim on all incomes, and returns to labor and capital ("the wage line") can only be paid after ground rent is satisfied. Moreover, this ground rent represents unearned income. Property increases in value because of the growth of population, improvements in technology, or off-site improvements. None of these things are attributable to the land owner; he merely reaps where he did not sow. *All ground rent is economic rent.* Land costs nothing to keep it in production. Capital and labor are consumed in the process of production and must be replaced; the land endures.

Note that we are speaking of taxing only the ground rent; the improvements would not be taxed at all. The improvements to the property represent capital and labor, and their work should not be taxed. Only the ground rent, the portion provided by the community, would be taken, and taken at something close to 100 percent of its value. For example, if a given house costs $200,000, the price is really for two things, the house and the land underneath it. Say the land costs $40,000 and the house $160,000. The house, being a product of labor and capital, would not be taxed at all. The land would be taxed at its full rental value, say $4,000/year. If the owner were to make a large addition to the house of say, $50,000, the ground rent would not change and the addition would not be taxed. For some localities, $4,000 might sound like a high tax, but in every locality it would be a low tax if it were the only tax one pays.

This is not a new idea. It was the form of taxation favored by economists from Adam Smith to Milton Friedman. It was most famously popularized by Henry George, a name that is forgotten today, although he was the most well-known and popular of the economists of the late nineteenth and early twentieth centuries. Some measure of his popularity can be gathered from the fact that at his death, one hundred thousand people filed past his coffin, and thousands of others waited outside and could not get in to pay their last respects. Can you imagine the general public lining up to for the funeral of any other economist?

George's theory is often called a "single-tax" theory, because it reduces all taxes to ground rent alone. This is a misnomer, however, since it should be called a "no-tax" theory. A tax is a cost added to a price or subtracted from an income. A sales tax is added to the price, an income tax deducted from the income. And these taxes tend to get passed along to the final consumer. But the Georgist "tax" simply appropriates the income of the rentier or landlord, the person who lives off other people's work. Nor can this "tax" be passed along. Ground rent already tends to absorb all values over the margin of production; the price cannot be increased beyond this.

The major question is whether such taxes are just, whether the major burden of taxation should fall entirely on the rentier. Two points are important here: One is that the value of ground rent is due to the community, not the owner (chapter 9). It is but justice that the community be funded from its own natural revenues. The second point is that ground rent always represents *wealth without work,* which is the primary source of both economic inefficiency and economic injustice. Wherever one person gets wealth without work, another must provide work without wealth. Clearly this is unjust, but it is also inefficient. The maldistribution of incomes affects such technical measures as the velocity of money and the incentives to invest, and thereby destabilizes the economy. But further, it leaves the community without a source of revenue for public purposes; the community therefore has no choice but to go after the returns to labor and capital, which negatively impacts both. Taking the ground rents, however, impacts neither—any further than rent does, anyway. Therefore, we can assert that *ground rent is the natural income of a community.* Rent derives its power strictly from a legal claim to property; that is to say, it is a creation of government power, a power that recognizes no limits to property. But property, like any other natural thing, has natural limits.

And the natural limit to property is that one should profit from its use and not from mere ownership.

Taking ground rent would have profound macroeconomic consequences. For one thing, land speculation would be unprofitable. The only way to make money off of land would be to use it, to employ it in providing a useful good or service to one's neighbors. The whole problem with the speculative rent line and the resulting land bubbles and subsequent contractions would disappear. The economy would be far more stable. For another thing, wages and investment would get their full return; both are now burdened by both rents *and* taxes. Without taxes on either, the work and investment climate would be very much improved.

But Is It Enough?

Although many economists generally concede the superiority of ground rents, they also doubt that it is adequate, especially when the total government expenditures come to $5 trillion. In this critique, they are absolutely correct. It is unlikely that ground rents could support a government establishment that takes one-third of GDP, an amount that is growing, especially during this current crisis. But that is not so much a critique of the land tax as one of its greatest advantages. Under a land tax, the public revenues would be fixed and known. Government at all levels would be confined within the limits of their funding. But how much would that funding be, and is it adequate to a reasonable level of government?

Empirical studies are hard to come by, since local taxing authorities are not overly concerned with separating the price of the land from the price of the improvements. The best studies suggest that ground rent revenue would come to about 20 percent of GDP, or about 60 percent of funding at all levels of government.[1] This would certainly leave a big hole in the current level of government, but this might not be as big a problem as it appears at first glance. It would force government to consider what should be funded from general revenues, and what should come from user fees. We have already discussed how the highway system is an obvious example of an expense that can be moved from general revenues to tolls. But there are many items in the budget that are in fact services to particular clienteles. For example, the Food and Drug Administration is a service to the pharmaceutical firms, among others, and its entire budget should come from user fees. By cutting the bloated defense budget, going to debt-free money, eliminating useless departments such as education, charging public works to the properties that benefit from them, and like measures, the federal budget could easily be cut by 40 percent without compromising any current services.

I suspect that the same rules would apply to state and local governments. The lion's share of these budgets are consumed by an ever-more-expensive education system. However, while it is certainly a duty of government to ensure that every child has the same opportunities to get an education, there is no reason for the state to actually run any schools, a task which they do not do well. A system of vouchers to parents would likely bring both great diversity and great economies to the educational system, while allowing the public to recoup their investment by selling the schools and putting the land back on the land-tax rolls. Support for education should also include some modest support for the most economically efficient and natural method of education for the very young, that is, for homeschooling.

Political Effects

Political power tends to flow to the greatest funding source. When the federal government gained the power to tax incomes, power naturally flowed upward, so that today senators and presidents routinely handle matters that are best left to the town council or the statehouse. A land tax, however, is most efficiently collected at the local level. The apparatus for doing so is already in place, since localities collect property taxes, though under widely varying rules and rates. The rules and methods would have to be standardized across the nation. But a land tax would entirely change the nature of government in the United States. With taxes collected at the local level, and divided in a fixed proportion among local, state, and federal authorities, we can expect that power will begin to flow back to the states and cities. And with a fixed budget, it will be easier to confine the federal government within its constitutional limits.

The two great debates in a land-tax system will be how to split the revenues and which programs should be funded or subsidized from general revenues and which should be funded by user fees. As matters currently stand, states and cities have an incentive to "kick problems upstairs" to the federal government, where the money is. Relying on the federal budget allows local entities to claim a bigger share of the income taxes their citizens pay, and to isolate the local tax base from these responsibilities. But a land tax reverses these incentives; since the tax base is the same for all levels of government, only the division of the revenues is at issue. Local entities therefore have an incentive to accept greater responsibility and hence claim a greater share of the revenue.

Further, they have an ironclad argument when dealing with the federal government; they merely need to ask about any particular program, "Where in the Constitution is this authorized?" Of course, they have that argument today, but they are not inclined to use it because the funding argument will always trump the constitutional one. Under a land tax, both arguments will work in favor of the local entities. The land tax will therefore advance the distribution of power which is an essential part of distributism. It will also encourage leaders at all levels of government to offload as many programs as possible from general revenues to fee-based services.

The Land Tax and Distributism

In advocating the land tax, I am not advocating something without historical precedent or current practice. In fact, the majority of tax systems before the modern age were based on land. The English feudal system was essentially a land-tax system. And in the modern world, highly successful states like Singapore, British Hong Kong, and Taiwan are "Georgist" land-tax states (states that follow the single-tax theory of Henry George). However, these states also indicate the problem with the land tax. In theory, the value of land should be easy for the authorities to calculate, since there is always an active market in land. And this is true, so long as there are no tax implications in separating the price of land and the value of the improvements. Two problems arise: One is that since improvements are not taxed, there is an incentive to attribute as much value as possible to the improvements and as little as possible to the land. The second is that when land ownership or control is concentrated, the landowners exercise considerable influence in setting the rules. Thus, a "pure" land-tax system has been difficult to establish or maintain over time. It tends to degenerate into a mere property tax which is insufficient to fund the state and becomes supplemented by income and other taxes (although usually at a much lower rate than in non-Georgist states). Large landowners like to see other taxes, because these are easier to avoid or to pass on to the final consumer.

The land tax works best where ownership is well divided and property not concentrated into large estates or tracts, in other words, in a distributist state. With land well distributed, political power is also well distributed, and the incentives to "off-load" the taxes from land to labor are decreased. On the other hand, a distributist state needs the land tax to prevent property from reaggregating; without a land tax, the distributist state tends to degenerate into a capitalist state, and no one is better off. Therefore, a Georgist polity needs distributism for its implementation; distributism needs Georgism to maintain itself.

Other Forms of Economic Rent

Land rent is not the only form of economic rent, even if it is the most obvious and important one. Other rents arise from monopoly or oligopoly control of economic resources, from patents, from control of scarce commodities, and from occupying positions of power within large institutions, mainly the corporation. This rent manifests itself in various ways, but the most obvious way is suspiciously high returns to capital. To deal with these other forms of rent, I suggest that the corporate income tax be maintained, but only assessed when the return to capital gets to be outsized. I suggest that we adopt some figure as a "normal" return to capital, say 8 percent, and start a modest tax when double that return is reached (16 percent), a high tax when it is tripled (24 percent), and a punitive tax when it is quadrupled (32 percent).

This would not impact the willingness to invest. While in general high returns attract investment, such returns, like every other economic quantity, have a "marginal utility." At some point, higher returns do not attract additional capital, and at a higher rate, the returns actually act as a perverse incentive to discourage further investment. This is especially true in monopolies or oligopolies. When returns are so high, why invest to increase the supply and thereby lower the returns?

In the same vein, high-level executives often collect an economic rent in the form of perversely high salaries and bonuses. These salaries seem to be paid whether or not the enterprise is successful, and indeed some of the highest bonuses are paid for failure, such as when a CEO with a "golden parachute" is fired. These bonuses come out of the rewards that rightfully belong to the workers or the investors. One or two generations ago, a CEO would typically make twenty to forty times what the line worker made; now CEO salaries run three hundred to five hundred times that of the line worker. The simplest solution is to require corporations to pay a tax penalty for such salaries. When a salary reaches some multiple of the line worker's salary, say forty times, the company would pay at least a modest tax, a tax that at some point, say two hundred times the average, becomes punitive, in the 75–90 percent range. Note that this tax would be on the company, not the executive. It would entirely change the nature of the negotiation with that executive, would be certain, and would be easier to collect.

Externalities

Aside from wealth without work (economic rent), the other great economic evil occurs when some portion of the costs of a transaction is forced on some third persons who are not a party to the transaction. Firms, and especially large corporations, do their best to externalize as many of their costs as possible. The obvious example of an externality is pollution, by which a company treats the common air, streams, and ground as a free sewer. This sewer carries no cost to the company, but the surrounding communities pay the cost in declining health, increased medical expenses, and shortened lifespans.

Externalities take many forms. One common form is subsidized infrastructures. The "free" transportation systems, for example, are actually subsidies to businesses that depend on wide distribution and supply networks. These subsidies work to the disadvantage of local businesses and suppliers, because they unfairly lower the transportation costs of national and international competitors. "Big-box" stores like Wal-Mart could likely not survive if their transportation costs were not subsidized. This is especially true since the greatest amount of damage to roadbeds is done by large trucks. If there were weight-based tolls for using the roads, it is likely that the Wal-Mart model would simply be uncompetitive with local and regional producers and retailers.

Externalities distort the price system and give companies that can externalize their costs a competitive advantage over those who cannot. As it works out in the real world, it is large, international companies that can more easily take advantage of externalized costs, leaving small and local competitors at a disadvantage.

Aside from going to fee-based services, like tolls, government should use its taxing power to force companies to internalize all of their costs. The current "big idea" for controlling pollution is "cap-and-trade" systems. But such systems convert pollution into a property right, and then give the right to the wrong people, to the polluters rather than those harmed by the pollution. Clearly, if you want more of a thing, then simply turn it into a "right," especially a marketable right. You may take it for granted that the producers can produce more forms of pollution, and therefore more property rights, faster than you can print the new deeds. The best method is a scale of taxes on pollution that increase over time so as to "encourage" a firm to internalize all of its costs.

In general, government should be vigilant to detect and eliminate externalities. No price system can function properly if firms are freely allowed to externalize their costs either to government budgets or to the public "commons."

But Should We Cut the Budget?

We have assumed throughout this discussion that cutting government expenditures and eliminating economic rent and externalities are *good* things. The reality, however, is a bit more complex. The current industrial system actually *depends* on large government expenditures, economic rent, and the ability to externalize costs. So while cutting the budget in the abstract would be a good thing, in reality it would destroy the current system of industrial production and global trade.

So before we take our scalpel in hand to perform surgery on the budget, we need to understand what we are doing and where we are going. We need to couple fiscal reform with a reform of the industrial system itself. Otherwise, our surgery may be successful but the patient will die. What a new industrial system could look like—one not dependent on government largesse—is the subject of the next chapter.

16

Distributism and Industrial Policy

Can the Patient Be Saved?

It is clear to everyone that the world economy is undergoing a deep crisis. The question on everybody's mind is whether this is just a normal part of the so-called business cycle, or whether it represents something more profound, perhaps even the end of that form of capitalism as it has existed for the better part of the last century. Have we just caught a cold, or do we have cancer? I hope the answer is the former; I fear it is the latter.

If it is the former, then it is likely that some form of government stimulus is the proper remedy, and as much as all sides may debate the particulars, they all agree on the medicine. There is good reason to believe in this medicine: it has worked well and often since the end of World War II. Indeed, our economy has become dependent on huge government expenditures to remain in balance, and these temporary imbalances can be cured as they have been cured: by a little jiggling of the monetary and fiscal policy levers. If this is the case, then we will soon recover and go on as we have.

There is a stronger reason, however, to believe that it will not work as it has in the past, namely because it hasn't worked for the past eight years. The fact is, the economy has been operating under an extraordinary stimulus package since 2001. Think on this: George W. Bush took all the debt we accumulated between the time of Andrew Jackson (the last time the debt was paid off) up through Bill Clinton, *and doubled it.* He added $5 trillion to the national debt, a considerable stimulus by any measure. And in 2009, considerably more than one trillion dollars was added to the federal debt, not to mention the trillions that were created by the Federal Reserve System to inject "liquidity" into the banking system.

Throughout it all, the economy remained anemic and then fell. And while its fate remains in the balance, there seems to be no real source of growth on the horizon, save for government spending. Indeed, even the "good years" were driven mainly by a housing bubble created not by any real growth, but by a compliant Fed and greedy financiers. An expansion of housing should be driven by an increase in wages, but median wages in this period actually fell. Hence, I think it reasonable to believe that what hasn't worked won't work; another $800 billion, or even another $5 trillion will not do the trick. The old reliable system will not work any longer, and no amount of medicine can revive it. The system must change or die, or must change after it dies. Change is inevitable; death is optional.

The problem lies not with the banking system—although it has its problems—but with the industrial and farming systems, which actually create wealth. All other economic enterprises depend on these. Without fixing the industrial system, all other fixes will be either meaningless or, at best, temporary. Here we will look at the problems of the current system, and how distributism responds to these problems.

The "Supply-Push" Industrial System

While we may think of the current industrial system as a natural or eternal part of capitalism, it is in fact of relatively recent vintage. Indeed, when Adam Smith wrote about "the invisible hand" in the eighteenth century, he assumed an economy of small and mostly local producers, none of which had any market power, and hence no way to substantially alter the competitive outcomes. Most firms, save a few dealing with commodities that were traded internationally, had an incentive to remain small and employ as little fixed-capital as possible.[1] But all that began to change in the nineteenth century, especially in the second half, with the development of the railroads. For the first time mass marketing over large areas became practical. The best way to take advantage of this new system was with highly expensive, special-purpose machinery. This made the capital employed in production very large, which meant that finance became more critical to the economy than ever before. Those without access to large amounts of capital had little chance of competing. By the late nineteenth century, a new form of organization had appeared, the "M-form corporation" ("M" for multidivisional) which spread all phases of production, often for very diverse products, across many divisions of the firm, while imposing a hierarchical structure to keep track of so many diverse functions.

All of this resulted in firms of tremendous economic and political power. This power replaced the invisible hand of Adam Smith with the all-too-visible hand of managers and government. Firms were now not price-*takers*, as in Smith's model, but price-*makers*. They could drive out smaller competitors, to be sure, but they could also drive down the price of labor. But when you drive down the price of labor, while increasing its productive capacity, you run into the problem that is usually called "overproduction" but is really "underpayment." By 1890, the system was already plagued with constant "overproduction" problems.

This structure is often called the "Sloanist" model, because it was perfected by Alfred Sloan, the legendary chairman of General Motors from 1923–46. Kevin Carson describes the model this way:

> The only way to keep the unit costs of such machinery down is large-batch production to utilize full capacity, and then worrying about making people buy it only afterward (commonly known as "supply-push distribution.") So Sloanist industry, under "Generally Accepted Accounting Principles," produces goods to sell to inventory, regardless of whether there are orders for it or even of whether the product works, and has an astronomical recall rate. It follows a business model based on consumer credit and planned obsolescence to keep the wheels running. As Ralph Borsodi described it, the push distribution system "amounted to making water run uphill." The overall logic of the system is that instilled by hypnopaedic suggestion in *Brave New World*: "Ending is better than mending." "The more stitches, the less riches."[2]

In other words, what the system actually manufactures is landfill, objects that spend as little time as possible in the hands of consumers as useful *products* while on their journey to the dump as useless *garbage*. Thus, the production model requires a consumerist model; we must be constantly taught, through expensive, manipulative, and unrelenting propaganda (advertising) that our happiness lies not in persons, but in things, and not merely in *things*, but in constantly *new* things. The old is icky; worse, it is unfashionable. Only by constantly buying what we don't need or already have can the system sustain itself; the size of the garbage dump becomes the true measure of our "wealth."

To solve the problem of overproduction, governments have resorted to growing the public sector to supplement demand. This is has been the greatest impetus behind not only the growth in government in the twentieth century, but also the extension of its imperialist and globalist reach in an effort to find, and force our way into, ever-new markets, as well as to guarantee sources of cheap labor and raw materials.

After World War II, the system reached some balance as the forces of the corporations, the government, and unions tended to balance each other out, and were sufficient, for a time, to keep wages high enough to absorb all the production, with some help from government spending. Since the 1970s, however, productivity has exploded while median wages have stagnated. A vast gap opened up between the goods available for sale and the purchasing power necessary to absorb them. Markets could not be cleared. The obvious way to solve this problem is to fix the wage system. Without a just wage—without the worker getting a fair claim to his portion of the output through his wages—there is insufficient purchasing power to clear the markets. But rather than fix the wage system, the economy has relied on consumer credit; those with too much money simply lend it to those with too little, and at usurious rates. This solves the problem in the short term, but it makes the long-term problem worse. Because of high interest, more and more capital gathers at the top, and the day of reckoning is deferred, but not deterred.

The consumer's problem becomes the *investor's dilemma*; without sufficient purchasing power in the mass of men, the pool of good investments shrinks, and the investor is forced to turn to pure speculation. He finds his portfolio full of exotic instruments he no longer understands. And what he primarily doesn't understand is that these instruments are not "investments" at all; that is, they do not provide funds to businesses to expand production. Rather, they are pure bets on the direction of some market, such as the housing market. Further, the excess capital tends to encourage leveraging; that is, investors lend huge amounts to other investors who place it in speculative instruments, which are themselves dependent on an increasingly troubled productive sector. What you have is a dense network of highly leveraged bets that depend on other bets that depend on an increasingly shaky productive sector. The bets are so highly intertwined that a failure in one sector endangers every other sector. That is how a failure in a relatively minor market, like subprime mortgages, can bring down the entire credit system.

Meanwhile in the productive sectors of the economy, the combination of an oversupply of capital and an underfunded consumer makes it difficult for businesses to increase their profits. In an effort to improve their margins, they start by firing their workers and end by firing their machinery; increasingly, the productive sectors move actual production overseas, leaving only a shell in the home country responsible for accounting, coordination, and marketing. Production is distributed, but legal control remains centralized. They invest their capital not in expanding production, since the consumer can't absorb any more production anyway, but in acquiring other companies to eliminate competition. The result is that ownership is increasingly concentrated in vast collectives known as corporations, even as production is distributed around the globe.

The argument in favor of the M-form megacorporation has centered on the "economies of scale" that such large organizations can obtain. However, while there are some economies of scale, these are vastly outweighed by the diseconomies of scale; mere size brings great problems. But mere size also brings great power, and it is this power that interferes with the free market and hides the inefficiencies. Corporations can command the resources of government to obtain subsidies and favorable tax treatment, and they can raise barriers to competition through regulations whose main purpose is to raise the entry cost to small and more efficient competitors. Without the subsidies to hide the diseconomies and the barriers to keep out competition, the megacorporation would not be a viable enterprise.

The Corporation as a Planned Economy

Economic literature is full of critiques of the socialist planned economies, all of which highlight the difficulties of bureaucratically allocating resources in the absence of a real market. But as it happens, all of these critiques can be applied equally to the modern corporation. After a certain size, the M-form corporation becomes indistinguishable from a planned economy, and converts what should be a "free market" enterprise into a bureaucratic structure that suffers from all the problems of a socialist state, with none of the benefits. To see how this happens, let us examine these problems in more detail.[3]

Lack of an Internal Market

In a corporation of any size, there is an enormous internal trade in goods and services. The outputs for one division are the inputs to another, and services such as accounting, computing, and marketing are offered across divisional boundaries.[4] But there is no market for these goods and services. In general, each division does not have a choice about which products and services to purchase and to whom they will sell their product. Yet, without a market, how does one know how to price products or how to allocate resources? The answer is that products are priced, and resources allocated, bureaucratically, by administrative decisions. Managers often find that their main job is to constantly fight the "battle of the budget" since it is the administrative process, and not the market, that determines their success. Readers will recognize this as the primary critique of a socialist economy, but one that fits equally the corporate economy. But a bureaucrat, public or private, can only make decisions as good as the information he receives. And here we encounter another problem endemic to both the corporate and socialist systems.

Information costs

In a large organization with a highly complex structure, there is a separation of knowledge from work and a distribution of information spatially across many offices that may be separated by thousands of miles. But before any decisions can be made, this information must be gathered, processed, assimilated, and judged. Further, the separation of knowledge from work removes the information from any context, and as the people who must use the information have little knowledge of the work they remotely supervise, the ability to judge information gets lost. It is not that such organizations lack information; quite the contrary, they are inundated by it. But it is like doing a Google search and coming up with millions of websites, only a few of which are relevant. It is impossible to know in advance which websites have the needed content. Unfortunately, in a hierarchical structure, power relationships tend to determine the content; there is always the danger that a "rank-based" logic will prevail. Managers, intent on advancement, tend to supply the information they know their superiors want to hear, rather than the information they ought to hear. Large organizations tend, therefore, to become systematically stupid.

All of this imposes high information costs. But no matter how many resources are devoted to information gathering and analysis, there is no way to ensure the completeness, accuracy, or relevance of the information.

Agency Problems

In a socialist economy, the officers of the state are supposed to run an economy that is "owned" by the people and act as their agents. But in practice, the socialist managers become the effective owners of the system, constituting a privileged group with their own interests. No matter how democratic the political system, the public at large generally lacks the information necessary to manage large enterprises. The same critique, however, applies to corporate management. The board of directors is supposed to act as the agent of the stockholders, and the managers as agents of the board. But as with the socialist collective, the managers of corporate collectives become the de facto owners.

John Bogle, the founder and former president of the Vanguard Funds, has documented the ways in which the top managers have constituted themselves as a new class that appropriates to itself all the privileges of ownership without any of the risks.[5] These top managers appropriate to themselves outsized rewards that should, by right, go to the owners and the workers. How can they do this? Ownership of a business once designated active control of that business, but now, as John Bogle notes,

> The position of ownership has changed from that of an active to that of a passive agent. The owner now holds a piece of paper representing a set of rights . . . but has little control. The owner is practically powerless to affect the underlying property through his own efforts . . . the "owner" of industrial wealth is left with a mere symbol of ownership while the power, the responsibility and the substance which have been an integral part of ownership in the past are being transferred to a separate group in whose hands lies control.[6]

In other words, "ownership" itself no longer has the meaning in the corporation that it does with any other form of property. "Ownership" has been attenuated to a mere claim to whatever portion of the profits that the directors care to distribute, and the right to vote for these directors. This "right," however, from the standpoint of the average shareholder, is more formal than actual. In practice, the costs of running a campaign against board members is prohibitively high, and the right to vote means little to the average stockholder, who rarely exercises it. In absence of active owners, the executives become the de facto owners of the firm. The corporation becomes, in effect, a mass of unowned capital appropriated by the managers. This new class tends to push the burdens and risks of work downward, and the rewards upwards.

The Divorce of Technical from Entrepreneurial Knowledge

Socialist planners prided themselves on their technical expertise and their deference to engineering talent. As their critics point out, however, while technology provides us with an endless range of production possibilities, it is impossible to evaluate these possibilities without knowing the price of the inputs. Since so many of the inputs are internal to the corporation, and since the corporation benefits from so many public subsidies, it is impossible to say that one system is more "efficient" than another. One can easily point to engineering marvels, but one cannot say that they are economically efficient. For example, the distribution system built by Wal-Mart is certainly a technical achievement, but it depends on subsidized transportation costs. Without these subsidies, would the system aid or bankrupt the company? Neither the engineer nor the entrepreneur can answer such a question in absence of market prices.

Regarding this phenomenon, Kevin Carson, a researcher for the Center for a Stateless Society, notes:

Fully rational decisions are possible only if the knowledge of the relative value of inputs is combined with knowledge of how those inputs are to be used internally. The separation of ownership of capital from the knowledge of the production process leads to decisions divorced from reality. The same is true of the separation of management from the direct involvement in the production process, and the accountability of management to absentee owners rather than to workers.[7]

For these reasons—and for many others—the modern corporations form, in the words of David Friedman, "indigestible lumps of socialism" in what is supposed to be a free-market system. Like any socialism, the system becomes increasingly dependent on state power and subsidies.

The Distributist Alternative

This critique would be pointless if distributism had no alternatives to offer. And the distributist alternatives would not be credible unless they were on the ground and working in both large- and small-scale manufacturing. As it turns out, the distributist offers not abstract panaceas, but systems which are on the ground and functioning, systems which any interested party may examine for their effectiveness. One such system is the distributive economy of Emilia-Romagna in Italy. As Kevin Carson describes it:

> The closest existing model for sustainable manufacturing is Emilia-Romagna. In that region of 4.2 million people, the most prosperous in Italy, manufacturing centers on "flexible manufacturing networks" of small-scale firms, rather than enormous factories or vertically integrated corporations. Small-

scale, general-purpose machinery is integrated into craft production, and frequently switches between different product lines. It follows a lean production model geared to demand, with production taking place only to fill orders, so there's no significant inventory cost. Supply chains are mostly local, as is the market. The local economy is not prone to the same boom-bust cycle which results from overproduction to keep unit costs down, without regard to demand. Although a significant share of Emilia-Romagna's output goes to the export market, its industry would suffer far less dislocation from a collapse of the global economy than its counterparts in the United States; given the small scale of production and the short local supply chains, a shift to production primarily for local needs would be relatively uncomplicated. The region's average wage is about double that of Italy for a whole, and some 45% of its GDP comes from cooperatively owned enterprises.[8]

The salient points of this analysis concern distributed and flexible manufacturing, the use of small-scale, general-purpose machinery, the gearing of production to demand ("demand-pull" rather than "supply-push"), local supply chains, and widespread worker ownership. Let us look at these points in turn.

Flexible Manufacturing

Flexible manufacturing allows for the quick movement among different product lines as demands shift. This is difficult in the M-form corporation, where a new product line often involves setting up a new division complete with its own capital requirements, not to mention management overhead. Moreover, it is easier to integrate this sort of manufacturing with craft production, bringing about the best of both worlds. "Craft" no longer has to mean a trade-off between quality and price, between single-piece and mass production.

General-Purpose Machinery

The use of general-purpose machinery means that the factory can shift easily from product line to product line, as demand dictates, without excessive retooling costs. The current system, which relies on product-specific machinery, cannot match this advantage. Moreover, such general-purpose machinery is already widespread. Most households already own quite a bit of it, and if you canvass any neighborhood, you are likely to discover a wealth of capital which can be joined together to produce a variety of products cheaply, efficiently, and locally.

Demand-Pull Production

Demand-pull manufacturing has a number of both economic and social consequences. Economically, it lowers the need for inventories, encourages the localization of those supply lines, and lessens the "boom-bust" cycle. But socially, it relies less on advertising to move goods. Currently, consumers are the victims of nonstop propaganda which appeals to their basest instincts. It is no more than commercial pornography, but it is necessary to the supply-push problem. This propaganda is especially directed at children, who must be socialized to the culture of consumerism if the current system is to survive. Demand-pull production assumes a closer relationship between supply and demand. It does require that there be a closer relationship between the producer and the consumer, that is, it relies on a *social* relationship rather than just an *economic* one. It also assumes general-purpose machinery which can be switched easily between different products, so that it does not rely on huge demand in one product to be cost-effective, the way that special purpose machinery does, which provides for a richer variety of production and a wider range of products.

Local Supply Chain

Local supply chains greatly lower costs and increase the utility of any firm to its own region. We have convinced ourselves that it is more "efficient" to ship a tomato two thousand miles before we eat it, or to ship parts from the other side of the world. But obviously, there is something wrong with that equation, and even the most dedicated "flat-earther" would concede that local supply is better than remote, all other things being equal.

Since the manufacturing is divided up among largely local firms that are selling to one another and to the public, the system is free-market and all the inputs are priced at their market price. This means that correct engineering, product, and marketing decisions can be made and resources allocated much more efficiently than in the internal socialism of the M-form corporation.

Widespread Worker Ownership

Widespread ownership overcomes the problems of the division of capital, management, and labor, and of the division between technical and entrepreneurial knowledge. Workers are no longer commodified cogs in an economic machine, but in control of their own destiny because they are the owners of their own properties, be it property in land, machinery, or skills. The problems associated with the division of ownership from work and management from knowledge of the production process are overcome. Moreover, a sense of community is encouraged and strengthened. And in the final analysis, this is the real purpose of an economy. It is never about just making piles of money, but about creating real wealth that supports real families and real communities.

Scalability

The M-Form corporation depends on gargantuan size to achieve its power, and thereby opens up a gap between business and "big business," two very different kinds of enterprises with two very different effects on the market. The distributed model has also shown itself to be effective in large-scale manufacturing (as we shall see in the next chapter) but it is also scalable down to the level of the family firm, or even the single individual. Indeed, the distributed model allows people to take advantage of the capital they have, but which is currently unused. For example, one can use one's own kitchen and spare room to open up a small restaurant or lunch counter. Indeed, it is only the oppressiveness of zoning laws, regulations, and the need for extensive tax accounting that keeps this from being more common than it is.

Now, one can debate as long as one wishes the efficacy of the distributive system. However, there is one group that has decided in favor of distributism, and that is the manufacturers themselves. For the past twenty years, they have been busy creating a perverse simulacrum of a distributed system. They have realized that it is no longer profitable to hold expensive machinery, and have distributed their plants throughout the world, outsourcing the work to third-world entrepreneurs who take all the risks of ownership. At the same time, the corporation relies on cheap transportation and legal ownership of the patents to maintain control of the end product. In today's industrial system, it is considered somewhat vulgar to actually own a factory when all that is needed is to own the brand.[9] This is the "Nike" system, where the "product" is not the shoe but the "swoosh" on the shoe. Indeed, Nike itself makes nothing but patents and advertisements; actual shoes are made in sweatshops. But the advertising allows Nike to sell a shoe with a dollar in direct labor costs for one hundred dollars.

This sounds like a good business, but actually the company sows the seeds of its own destruction. Management guru Thomas Peters gushes that some 90 percent of a product's value is not in material or labor costs, but in "intellectual property." What this means is that the corporation is able to exercise control through the patent laws. It will not take much, however, for the actual factories to decide that the patent has no moral or economic justification. They will tear off the "swooshtika" and discover that they can sell their product locally for one-tenth of the price while paying their workers three times the wage. As the current economic order disintegrates, the corporations are likely to find that they have set in place everything necessary for their own replacement.

And that is good news.

17

Distributism and the Health Care System

Distributism would be of little practical use if it could not provide useful answers to practical problems of the type we face practically everyday. I believe distributism does indeed provide a useful set of tools to analyze these problems and to devise useful solutions. But the proof of this claim can only come in the analysis of an actual problem. For this example of distributist analysis, I choose the American health care system, which is experiencing great difficulties, difficulties for which no one has yet devised a workable solution.

Some sign of these difficulties is shown by the fact that in 2007, the United States spent 16.2 percent of its GDP on health care, up from 8 percent in 1975.[1] Of this amount, the government pays about 46 percent. Compare this with Great Britain, where they spend about half that amount, or 8.4 percent of the GDP (2006).[2] In other words, the United States spends almost as much in public money as the English do in total, yet we do not have universal health care. We spend more in private funds than the English do in total, yet we do not have a free-market system. We spend more than any other country in the world on health care, but we have neither a truly public nor a truly private system. Rather, we have a complicated contraption that combines the worst features of capitalism and socialism. And for all the money we spend, we leave a large percentage of the population without insurance: 15.3 percent in 2007 (about forty-six million people and that number has risen by at least four million in the last year due to our economic problems). Further, even people who have insurance often find that it is inadequate, and a medical emergency leaves them with crushing debts. The insurance companies maintain large staffs whose only job is to deny as many claims as possible; indeed, their compensation is not based on how accurately they assess claims, but solely on how many they deny. Any claims adjuster who fairly assesses claims will quickly find himself unemployed.

Spending twice as much on health care might be justified if the results were significantly better. Yet the opposite is true. By every objective measure, we do far worse when compared to other industrialized nations. In terms of life expectancy, infant mortality, preventable diseases, and many other categories, the United States falls far behind Japan, Canada, Western Europe, and nearly all the other industrialized nations of the world.

The problem is not only the large share of the GDP that the system consumes, but also the continuing growth of that share. Over the last ten years, the growth in health care expenditures as a percentage of the GDP averaged 1.86 percent per year. Even during this current recession, the cost of health care has been the only thing that is growing. Obviously, this cannot continue; sooner or later the system must fall of its own weight, and my guess is that day is coming sooner rather than later. Nor does the recently passed (and misnamed) "Health Care Bill" fix the situation; rather, it adds thirty million new customers for health insurance without adding any new doctors, hospital beds, or clinics.

The increased pressures on the supply side are likely to push prices up even faster.

Some Possible Causes

Of the myriad of possible causes cited for this phenomenon, two are often given great weight in the discussion: improved technology and an aging population. However, there are serious problems with both of these explanations. Concerning improvements in technology, it is certainly true that there have been great advances in medicines and machinery. However, improvements in technology normally lower costs, not raise them. Health care is the only industry where an executive could get away with saying, "Our technology has vastly improved, therefore we are far less efficient." That being said, there is a case where improved technology actually raises costs; it is where the technology is provided under monopoly conditions. We will discuss this further in a moment.

An aging population seems a more plausible explanation, seeing that the problems of aging tend to be more chronic and expensive than those of easily repaired youth. However, this cannot be the full explanation, since aging is not a problem unique to the United States. All of the developed countries have similar demographics—or worse—yet still spend far less than the United States. So by itself, aging cannot be the problem. There is something unique about the American situation, however, which raises the costs of aging; namely, senior health care insurance is socialized while care for most of the rest of the population is not. This means that the elderly can outbid the young and middle-aged in competing for scarce medical resources, thereby raising the costs for everybody. There is, in effect, a socialized system competing with a private system (more or less), and the socialized system seems to have endless resources, since they are the resources of the United States government.

The recently passed health insurance bill merely complicates this situation. There is now a partially private, partially public *insurance* system that pays a largely privatised health care system. The "public" and "private" portions of this system will interact in complex and unpredictable ways. But the underlying price pressures are not addressed, and are likely only to get worse.

Many other causes are often cited: the cost of malpractice insurance, immigration, fragmentation, greed, regulation, and so forth. While each of these may play a role, they are not—individually or collectively—sufficient to explain the rapid and continuing rise in costs.

Free Market vs. Socialist?

The debates on this issue usually take place within the framework of "free market" vs. "socialized" medicine, yet the system we have is at the same time neither and both. It cannot be a free-market system because the supply of medicine and medical services is limited by licenses and patents. Milton Friedman advocated abolishing the licensing of doctors altogether. Friedman argued that medical licenses restrict the supply of doctors and thereby raise the cost. He believed that the free market would judge medical competence better than any license board, rewarding the competent doctors and punishing the incompetent.

The problem with Friedman's argument is that we have already tried that. Right into the early twentieth century, doctors were unlicensed; they took perhaps one or two years at a medical college, usually a for-profit institution run by local doctors who lectured at the college. After their course of lectures, and without ever having touched a microscope or a cadaver, they set up as doctors. The results were disastrous, as became evident in the great Spanish influenza pandemic of 1918; the level of medical training was simply inadequate to deal with the crisis. After that disaster, the move to improve education and require licenses gained public support to produce the system we have today, a system largely controlled by the American Medical Association (AMA).

Further, a free-market solution depends on the availability of information and the ability to judge that information. In comparing doctors, information about them is hard to come by, and even if I had such information, I would not be able to make an informed judgment. And if I am having a heart attack, I am in no position to do the comparison shopping that a free market requires.

Yet for all that, Friedman has a point. By limiting the number of doctors, we restrict the supply and raise the cost. Further, because of the high training requirements required for the license, the education of a doctor is long, arduous, and expensive. New doctors are frequently burdened with huge education loans, and setting up a practice requires a huge capital investment. This forces doctors to act more like businessmen than medical professionals; they have to turn a large profit just to break even on both their costs and the amount of income forgone while they were getting their educations. And it has frequently been charged that the AMA restricts the number of "slots" in medical schools so as to further restrict supply.

Licenses are not the only problem in making medicine a free-market service. A greater problem results from patents for medicines and medical technology. A patent is a government-granted monopoly right which gives the patent holder the exclusive right to manufacture some particular product. Currently, patents run twenty years, during which the patent holder may place any price he chooses on his product, and he usually chooses a monopoly price. Monopoly pricing is the antithesis of free-market pricing. A free market, in theory at least, prices products to produce the highest possible amount of goods at the lowest possible price; the equilibrium point between supply and demand, under conditions of perfect competition, guarantees the lowest practical price to the buyer and the lowest practical return to the producer. But none of this is true under monopoly conditions. The producer supplies the least amount of product for the greatest possible price, and in the case of medicines, it is like selling water to people dying of thirst in the desert: they will pay any price to save their lives.

Monopoly pricing also has another and more insidious effect. In a competitive market, price serves as an allocation signal. A price that is too high will leave some goods unsold; a price that is too low will result in a shortage of goods. The market will provide the proper signals to producers telling them how much product to supply to the market and at what price. But monopoly destroys this mechanism; the monopolist may demand a share of whatever funds are supplied to a given market, and the more funds supplied, the higher the prices go without increasing the supply of the product. This is sufficient to explain why medical expenses consume an ever increasing share of the GDP without increasing the number of people covered. More funding means only higher prices, not more actual goods supplied. But as the monopolists claim an ever-larger share of the total GDP, the system must sooner or later collapse.

The argument for patents is that they increase innovation; without the prospect of great wealth, people will have no incentive to develop the miracle drugs and marvelous technology that we enjoy. In other words, for the sake of science and progress, we must accept monopolies.

Health Insurance

It is often suggested that insurance can function as a middle term between the market and socialism. However, this involves a misunderstanding of what insurance is. Insurance can only be a means of cost averaging; some must pay too much and others too little, but one way or another, the cost must be paid by the users, which, in a monopolistic market, will price many out of the market. Healthy purchasers will seek plans that eliminate as many "risky" applicants as possible; they will seek the safest "risk pool," which is reflected by the lowest cost. People with higher risks will be placed in higher risk pools with higher prices, which will price many out of the market. So nothing is gained towards a universal, affordable system.

Further, insurance works differently in a monopolistic market. Cars and homes can be efficiently insured because the home- and car-repair businesses operate under relatively free markets, which means that insurers can rely on the market to control costs. Insurance will have some inflationary effects, as people perform repairs they might otherwise have deferred, but in general the effects are mild. This is not true in the presence of monopolies; the monopolistic market cannot be relied on to control costs, quite the opposite: the more money supplied to a monopoly, the more the prices will rise. This in turn raises the cost of insurance, which drives more people out of the market. The effect is that prices rise while coverage shrinks, or precisely the effects we are seeing in the real world.

Some have suggested that these problems will go away if we make insurance mandatory and universal, as in the Massachusetts Plan. However, a mandatory purchase is just another name for a tax; since everybody is required to purchase the product, it cannot really be a free market. Again, some argue that even though the purchases are mandatory, the system is still "free market" because of the variety of plans and prices provided. However, the price differences in the plans can only come from differences in coverage. Some will cover more, and some less; some will deny more claims, and others less. People will have to guess in advance what diseases and medicines they are likely to need, and to the extent that they guess wrong—which is inevitable—they will be uninsured. You will have, essentially, the same situation we have today but in a different form: instead of the insured and uninsured, you will have the fully insured and the partially insured, with partial insurance being the equivalent of noninsurance for many situations.

Again, some will counter that the government can require all the plans to cover the same things. However, a standard, compulsory plan is no different from socialized medicine, and is likely to be a good deal less efficient. There are likely to be high expenses for profit and marketing, even though profits are not justified for compulsory purchases, and the "marketing" can be no more than an effort to convince people to buy the same product with a different label on it; it serves no useful purpose and only adds useless expense. Finally, there is likely to be duplication in administrative expenses. If all the companies are selling and administering the same plan, there is simply no reason to have multiple administrative organizations. In such a case, a "single-payer" system makes more sense.

Some will argue that Health Savings Accounts (HSAs) combined with catastrophic insurance will go a long way towards solving the problem. HSAs allow people to put a portion of their income in tax-free savings accounts, usually up to about six thousand dollars per family, to pay for ordinary medical expenses and then buy high-deductible policies to cover anything beyond that. The benefits are that people pay for most care from their own funds and are thus likely to make better use of the funds. At the same time, high-deductible policies are much cheaper. Between the two, great efficiencies are gained.

HSAs or some variation have been in place for many years, but have done little to address the underlying problems. The reasons are not hard to find. The first problem is that the people who are least able to afford insurance are also those who are least likely to have a surplus that they can save. In an economy that has seen a stagnant median wage for thirty years, even in the face of rapidly rising productivity, this should not be surprising. HSAs will not help the unemployed or the underemployed at all. Further, the majority of those who cannot afford any insurance are already in the lowest tax bracket, hence the tax advantages are minimal. And the majority of taxes that they do pay are the FICA taxes, and HSAs are not exempt from these. The greatest advantages of HSAs go to those who need them the least. A person in the lowest tax bracket, assuming he can save $6,000, might get a $600 tax advantage, but a person in the 35 percent bracket gets a $2,100 government benefit. Although the intentions behind HSAs are laudable, in effect they are mere subsidies to those who already have sufficient surplus.

Ending the Oligarchies and Monopolies

It should be clear that the vast majority of current thinking about the health-insurance problem does little to address the underlying causes of the dilemma. And this is odd because the mechanics of prices are well known and have been since the time of Aristotle. No competent economist of whatever school disputes these mechanics. There are two bedrock facts about any market system that we must confront:

1. You cannot lower prices without raising supply relative to demand.
2. You cannot raise the supply in the face of oligarchies and monopolies.

Therefore, the key to the problem is first to control or eliminate the monopolies. Without addressing this problem, the system will be as it is, and the "reform" will only make it worse; adding new funding and new demand to a monopoly system will force prices to rise. There can be no question, however, that a continuing stream of innovations have been provided under the patent regime, and medical licenses have guaranteed at least a minimum level of training for medical personnel. Is there any way to reform these systems and yet maintain their advantages?

The Problem of Patents

Contrary to received wisdom, patents are *not* necessary for research in any field. Even today in the medical field, 40 percent of research funds come from the government or from nonprofit organizations. Hence, even a sudden end to the patent system would not end medical research. What research does require is a reliable funding source, which can come more efficiently from manufacturing licenses than from patents; that is, when a firm develops a new medicine they get the right to license that product to any number of production firms. The licenses should be for a longer term than the current patents, which will provide research and development (R&D) firms with a much more secure revenue stream from which to fund further research. The license fee would be small relative to the current monopoly profits, but they would continue for a longer period of time, after which the product would enter the public domain and be appropriated by everybody.

Manufacturers, on the other hand, will have to compete on price and service, and will therefore have to find the most efficient ways to manufacture and distribute the medicines. The effect of such a license system would be to divide R&D and manufacturing firms. R&D firms would want as many companies as possible to distribute their product, and would have an incentive to keep the fees low. There may be a role for the government in setting the license fees.

If, however, the pharmaceutical firms insist on maintaining their current monopolies, then the only way to control costs is to have government set the prices. This is anathema to a free-market system. Monopolies, however, are the antithesis of the free market. And the monopoly cannot have it both ways: it cannot insist that the government enforce their monopoly rights while demanding that the government take no role in pricing. If they wish the government to withdraw from pricing, then the government should cheerfully agree, but it should also withdraw from enforcing their patents. This system of price controls already obtains in countries with a "single-payer" system. The government negotiates the price of the drugs with the manufacturers. This is why American drugs are usually cheaper in other countries than they are in America. The American taxpayer bears all the burdens of research, but gets none of the price benefits.

The Problem of Medical Licenses

Milton Friedman is undoubtedly right that medical licenses restrict the supply of medical services, and under the current system, this will not change. The current system, however, may be an overreaction to the lax standards of the nineteenth century. And any group that sets its own standards is likely to set them too high in order to limit supply and keep their income high.

I believe that we can drastically increase the supply of medical services—and therefore decrease the price—by providing a range of licenses: midwives, nurse practitioners, medical practitioners, medical doctors, and more advanced doctors of medicine. First-line care could easily be provided by nurse practitioners and midwives working in their own neighborhood clinics, perhaps under the general supervision of a medical practitioner or medical doctor. Another area where this applies is in orthodontics. There is no reason why anybody needs a degree in dentistry to install orthodontics; the work could be as safely performed by orthodonturists, and at a far lower cost. It is only the legal monopoly that dentists have on the business which keeps the prices so high, thereby denying this useful and normally affordable service to many poor people, while charging the rest of us unreasonable prices.

A series of licenses would provide another benefit. As things stand now, a student will spend most of his youth and all of his fortune in getting an M.D., and will still be left with staggering debts. Yet, he will have a degree in a profession he has not actually practiced. A series of licenses will provide the student with a career path by which he may alternate education with practice. He will have an income stream with which to finance his education, but he will also have practical experience to take to each successive layer of education. This will produce doctors who are more practiced.

Medical Guilds

It is not enough, however, to address supply and demand problems. All social goods, medical services included, are delivered by institutions, and the structure and control of these institutions will dictate the outcomes. If our social institutions are organized solely around the profit motive, as they are now, they will find clever ways of defeating any attempts to restrain their power to set prices. People who are only concerned with supply and demand are usually baffled by how easily the mechanism breaks down and monopoly and oligopoly take control. But the answer is not surprising: if profit is the only measure, then the entire institutional effort will be toward breaking down the limits on profit, the major limit being a truly free market. (See chapter 5 on mechanisms businesses use to defeat market pricing.)

This is not to say that there is anything wrong with the profit motive per se. Indeed, without making a profit, no firm or institution can be sure that it is delivering a useful product and correctly allocating its resources. But it is to say that a single measure—*any* single measure—is always self-defeating. As an analogy, suppose we designed cars solely on the basis of safety. We would indeed produce cars that were absolutely safe in nearly any circumstances. Such cars, however, would be so heavy and expensive that few people would want them. In the same way, a system where profit is the only measure will eventually fail even to make a profit. Other measures must come into play. But an institution solely devoted to profit cannot allow such measures. So what institutional framework should medicine have?

I believe that the answer lies in a well-tested institution from our past, and that institution is the *guild*. The guilds were associations of professionals in a given field who took responsibility for the training of their members and the quality and price of their products and services. They were the sole judges of the qualifications of their members, and had the power to set both standards and prices. What I propose is that we allow medical professionals to form guilds with the power to grant various licenses. They would be the sole judges of the qualifications required, and they would set the practice standards and prices. But most importantly, the guild would stand surety for its members. That is to say, when a patient had a complaint, he would sue not the doctor but the guild. The guild would be responsible for the competence and good conduct of its members.

You might ask, "Why would one doctor stand surety for another?" In fact, this is what already happens in malpractice insurance. Insurance is merely cost averaging. If the losses go up for one doctor, the rates for every other doctor in that insurance pool go up. But doctors have no control over who is in their insurance pool; the quack and the competent get thrown in the same insurance system, with the latter required to pay for the former. In a guild system, the guild would have a strong incentive to ensure the competence of their members and monitor their practice standards; they would want to weed out the incompetent or downgrade their licenses. The guild would purchase insurance for all its members, or even provide the insurance itself, thereby removing the profit motive and lowering the cost.

Since the guild would be the sole judge of the qualifications and practices of its members, there would be a greater diversity of practical approaches. The Guild of St. Luke, for example, might favor one approach to medicine, the Galen Guild might favor another, and natural competition and practical experience would be sufficient to discover the superior approach. And while it might be difficult for the public to judge one doctor against another, it would be easier to judge the performance of one guild versus another. Further, this also provides space for "alternative medicine." I have no way to judge whether such things as acupuncture or Chinese herbalism are medically valid. But when joined in a guild and required to stand surety for each of their members, practices which do have some value would likely thrive, even if conventional medicine does not, as yet, recognize their value. And if they have no value, it is likely that such practices would simply disappear because the insurance claims would bankrupt them. Likely the government would still have some minimal role to prevent outright quackery; they would not likely allow, for example, a Guild of Peach Pit Cure-Alls.

In addition to insuring their doctors, the guild would offer insurance to the public; that is, they could offer to treat people for a fixed annual fee. This would give the guilds an income stream, but also a great incentive to insure that small problems do not go untreated to become big problems. In other words, such health insurance would actually be concerned with insuring health rather than denying claims. Further, the guilds could be required to devote a certain amount of their resources to free or low-cost care for the impoverished or indigent. The government might play a role here in qualifying people as eligible for such reduced-cost treatment, and could even pay a part of the cost.

The guild would be empowered to establish its own clinics, its own training and education programs, its own pharmacies, labs, administrative structures, and whatever else is necessary to medical practice. This would also make it easier for medical professionals to enter practice without worrying about setting up the business and administration that consume so much of doctors' time today. The doctor, and every other member of the guild, would be the "owners" of the guild, and while they would certainly be interested in their own incomes, it would be impossible for that to be their sole interest, not so long as they are providing insurance to each other and to the public.

The Future of Reform

The current system, consuming 16 percent of GDP—and rising—is simply unsustainable. Moreover, the great burden it places on our businesses makes us uncompetitive in world markets, as we have discovered in the auto industry. The status quo is no longer an option. But here we come to a great conundrum: either we return to the chaos and quackery of the nineteenth century, or we move to a European-style socialist system, in which medical services are allocated by the state. European socialism has resulted in better overall health statistics and at least a *perception* of fairness in allocating services. However, socialism converts each person from being a citizen to being a ward of the state. Nevertheless, if one has a life-threatening illness or injury, one might prefer to be a live ward rather than a dead citizen.

But there is a great problem in establishing universal health care, whether by socialism or any other method; namely, there will be an additional fifty million persons in the system who are currently uninsured, plus the untold millions who are underinsured. This is a tremendous increase in demand with no corresponding increase in supply. Either there will be huge price increases, or the government will be forced to severely ration health care. Both courses of action are untenable, and the system will collapse before it gets started. Without increasing the supply, you cannot control the costs, and this is impossible without curtailing or eliminating the monopolies and oligarchies that currently restrict supply.

But if costs are brought under control by market forces, and the institutional problem is solved by the guild, then the problem of universal care will turn out to be a relatively easy one; providing medical insurance to all will be no more difficult than providing car or home insurance. No system of reform currently on the table addresses either the supply or the institutional problems. Instead, they all exacerbate both problems. It will become painfully clear that as we move towards universal care, we will increase the demand but leave the supply unchanged. This will result in disaster. I firmly believe that only a distributist analysis can give us the tools to look the problem squarely in the eye and provide rational solutions.

18

The Practice of Distributism

Somewhere, the Sage hath said, "Philosophy is easy; plumbing is hard." The Sage is correct: we should be suspicious of systems that exist only in the mind, but are never seen on the ground. It is only in the real world that they can be tested, and on those grounds alone we should take our stand. It is easy—too easy—to come up with abstract systems which are perfection itself; it is much harder to make them work. The problem with abstract theorizing is that creating theories is a selection process; one must decide what to leave in and what to take out. But one can never know that the right elements have been included without seeing how the system works in practice. Hence, practice alone is the only standard of judgment about social systems.

In chapter 2 we noted the failure of capitalism to live up to its own standards, to deliver what it promises. We noted that it always and everywhere ends up with a statist economy, ever more dependent on government interventions. But such a critique would ring hollow if distributism did not have its own practice that the capitalist could examine in the same way we have examined capitalism. Fortunately, there are many long-standing examples of distributist economies and practices, and their problems and successes can be examined in as much detail as you like; we can see whether the theory describes an actual practice, and whether the practice works as advertised. Here I will mention only the more prominent examples, and I invite the reader to examine them in greater detail for himself.

The Mondragón Cooperative Corporation (MCC)

Recently, the workers in the Fagor Appliance Factory in Mondragón, Spain, received an 8 percent cut in pay.[1] This is not unusual in such hard economic times. What is unusual is that *the workers voted themselves this pay cut.* They could do this because the workers are also the owners of the firm. Fagor is part of the Mondragón Cooperative Corporation (MCC), a collection of cooperatives in Spain founded over fifty years ago.

The story of this remarkable company begins with a rather remarkable man, Father José Maria Arizmendiarrieta, who was assigned in 1941 to the village of Mondragón in the Basque region of Spain. The Basque region had been devastated by the Spanish Civil War (1936–38); they had supported the losing side and had been singled out by Franco for reprisals. Large numbers of Basques were executed or imprisoned, and poverty and unemployment remained endemic until the 1950s. In Father José's words, "We lost the Civil War, and we became an occupied region."[2] However, the independent spirit of the Basques proved to be fertile ground for Father José's ideas. He took on the project of alleviating the poverty of the region. For him, the solution lay in the pages of the papal encyclicals *Rerum Novarum*, *Quadragesimo Anno*, and in the thinkers who had pondered the principles these encyclicals contained. Property, and its proper use, were central to his thought, as it was to Pope Leo XIII and to Belloc and Chesterton. "Property," Father José wrote, "is valued in so far as it serves as an efficient resource for building responsibility and efficiency in any vision of community life in a decentralized form."[3]

Father José's first step was the education of the people into the distributist ideal. He became the counselor for the Church's lay social and cultural arm, known as "Catholic Action," and formed the *Hezibide Elkartea,* The League for Education and Culture, which established a training school for apprentices. He helped a group of these students become engineers, and later encouraged them to form a company of their own on cooperative lines. The engineers agreed to do so, but had no specific plan or product in mind. In order to establish a factory, it was necessary to obtain a license from the government, which was not always cooperative toward the Basques. But when a nearby stove factory went bankrupt, they raised $360,000 from the community to buy it in 1955.[4] This first of the co-operatives was named *Ulgor,* which was an acronym from the names of the five students of Father José who were the founders. It was first organized as a conventional business because there was no legal form for cooperatives, nor would there be until 1959.

From such humble beginnings, the cooperative movement has grown to an organization that employs over 100,000 people in Spain, has extensive international holdings, has, as of 2007, 33 billion in assets (approximately U.S. $43 billion), and revenues of 17 billion. 80 percent of their Spanish workers are also owners, and the Cooperative is working to extend the cooperative ideal to their foreign subsidiaries.[5] 53 percent of the profits are placed in employee-owner accounts. The cooperatives engage in manufacturing of consumer and capital goods, construction, engineering, finance, and retailing. But aside from being a vast business and industrial enterprise, the corporation is also a social enterprise. It operates social insurance programs, training institutes, research centers, its own school system, and a university; and it does it all without government support.

Mondragón has a unique form of industrial organization. Each worker is a member of two organizations, the General Assembly and the Social Council. The first is the supreme governing body of the corporation, while the second functions in a manner analogous to a labor union. The General Assembly represents the workers as owners, while the Social Council represents the owners as workers. Voting in the General Assembly is on the basis of "one worker, one vote," and since the corporation operates entirely from internal funds, there are no outside shareholders to outvote the workers in their own cooperatives. Moreover, it is impossible for the managers to form a separate class which lords it over both shareholders and workers and appropriates to itself the rewards that belong to both; the salaries of the highest-paid employee is limited to eight times that of the lowest paid.

Mondragón has a fifty-year history of growth that no capitalist organization can match. They have survived and grown in good times and bad. Their success proves that the capitalist model of production, which involves a separation between capital and labor, is not the only model, and certainly not the most successful model. The great irony is that Mondragón exemplifies the libertarian ideal in a way that no libertarian system ever does. While the Austrian libertarians can never point to a working model of their system, the distributists can point to a system that embodies all the objectives of a libertarian economy, but only by abandoning the radical individualism of the Austrians in favor of the principles of solidarity and subsidiarity.

The Cooperative Economy of Emilia-Romagna

Another large-scale example of distributism in action occurs in Emilia-Romagna, the area around Bologna, which is one of twenty administrative districts in Italy. This region has a hundred-year history of cooperativism, but the co-ops were suppressed in the 1930s by the Fascists. After the war, with the region in ruins, the cooperative spirit was revived and has grown ever since, until now there are about eight thousand co-ops. They are of every conceivable size and variety. The majority are small- and medium-sized enterprises, and they work in every area of the economy: manufacturing, agriculture, finance, retailing, and social services.

The "Emilian model" is quite different from that used in Mondragón. While the MCC uses a hierarchical model that resembles a multidivisional corporation (presuming the divisions of a corporation were free to leave at any time), the Emilian model is one of networking among a large variety of independent firms. These networks are quite flexible, and may change from job to job, combining a high degree of integration for specific orders with a high degree of independence. The cooperation among the firms is institutionalized mainly in two organizations, the Emilia-Romagna Development Agency (ERVET) and the National Confederation of Artisans (CNA).

ERVET provides a series of "real" service centers (as opposed to the "government" service centers) to businesses which provide business plan analysis, marketing, technology transfer, and other services. The centers are organized around various industries; CITER, for example, serves the fashion and textile industries, QUASCO serves construction, and CEMOTOR serves earth-moving equipment. CNA serves the small *artigiani*, the artisanal firms with fewer than eighteen employees in which the owner works within the firm, and adds financing, payroll, and similar services to the mix.

We discussed in chapter 16 how the cooperatives work as an industrial model. Here let us only add that that the Emilian model is based on the concept of *reciprocity*. Reciprocity revolves around the notion of bidirectional transfers; it is not so much a defined exchange relationship with a set price as it is an expectation that what one gets will be proportional to what one gives. The element of trust is very important, which lowers the transaction costs of contracts and lawyers, unlike modern corporations, where such expenses are a high proportion of the cost of doing business. But more than that, since reciprocity is the principle that normally obtains in healthy families and communities, the economic system reinforces both the family and civil society, rather than working against them.

Space does not permit me to explore the richness of the Emilian model. I will simply note here some of its economic results. The cooperatives supply 35 percent of the GDP of the region, and wages are 50 percent higher than in the rest of Italy. The region's productivity and standard of living are among the highest in Europe. The entrepreneurial spirit is high, with over 8 percent of the workforce either self-employed or owning their own business. There are ninety thousand manufacturing enterprises in the region, certainly one of the densest concentrations per capita in the world. Some have called the Emilian model "molecular capitalism";[6] but whatever you call it, it is certainly competitive with, if not outright superior to, corporate capitalism.

Taiwan and the Land to the Tiller Program

In 1949, the Chinese Nationalists were defeated by the Communists and fled to the island of Formosa, now called Taiwan. The Taiwan that greeted the refugees was a feudal backwater. Mostly it was a nation of small sharecroppers paying rents of 50–70 percent of the crop. Most of the land was owned by members of twenty families. Further, since the returns on land were so high, there was little interest in investing in industry. In addition, Taiwan had to absorb two million refugees from the mainland and bear the costs of defense. It was expected that Taiwan would soon fall to the mainland Communists, because the Kuomintang had never proved very effective in controlling China. It was necessary to act quickly to reform Taiwan; it was the very failure to enact reforms which had made the Kuomintang unpopular in China and led to the victory of the Communists. They could not make the same mistake twice.

Effective control of the Orient was in the hands of General Douglas MacArthur, who happened to be a distributist. He worked out a plan of reform for Korea, Japan, and Taiwan. Here we deal just with the reforms in Taiwan. The basis of the plan is that the farmers who actually worked the land would come into possession. The landowners were forced to sell the land to their tenants at a price equal to two and one-half times the average crop. The money to buy the land was given to the farmers, who repaid it over ten years. Under this "land to the tiller" program, 432,000 families came into possession of their own land.

The results were dramatic. Farm production increased as farmers used more fertilizer, went to multiple cropping with as many as four crops each year and diversified production to higher-value but more labor-intensive crops. Production increased at an annual rate of 5.6 percent from 1953 through 1970. The farmers suddenly had something they never had before: relatively large amounts of disposable income. Now they needed a place to spend it. Providing products to buy would require an expansion of industry on the island, if the country were not to be dependent on imports.

Most of the payments to the landowners were not in the form of cash, but in bonds. These bonds were negotiable industrial bonds which the former landowners could then invest in any light industry they chose.[7] Indeed, there was nothing else they could do with the bonds; it was a case of "invest or die." The strategy was twofold: get capital, in the form of land, into the hands of farmers; get capital, in the form of industrial investment, into the hands of entrepreneurs. Note that the strategy provided both goods to buy and purchasers to buy them; it was a *binary* strategy, giving equal weight to production and consumption. A tremendous number of capitalists were created overnight: the former landowners, who previously had no interest in manufacturing, were converted into instant urban capitalists and had to find places to invest the proceeds from the lands sales; the landless peasants became proprietors. By this method, the government provided support to Taiwan's fledgling industrial base. But the fact that the actual companies to invest in were picked by the former landowners meant better investment decisions than if the government had tried to pick the winners itself. Industrial production expanded, giving the newly empowered peasants places to spend their money while buying *locally* produced goods.

We can see the Taiwanese experiment for the conjuring trick it was: the government sold land it didn't own, bought with money it didn't have, and financed industries that didn't exist; the government managed both to expand the consumer market and to provide the industrial production necessary to serve that market and serve it from local resources. There was no inflation because the money supply expanded at the same rate as production by a sort of automatic method. Redistribution allowed for expansion of the consumer base which allowed for expansion of the industrial base. It is not often in business and economics that one gets to see solutions which are elegant and beautiful, but certainly the "land to the tiller" program qualifies.

The results have been impressive, both in economic and social terms. Starting with crude products made in small workshops, Taiwan followed the industrial value-added food chain right up to shipbuilding, electronics, and every sort of industry. Taiwan has managed fifty years of high growth rates, increased equality, and low tax rates (comparatively). Unemployment was low to nonexistent through most of Taiwan's post war history. Before 2000, it rarely exceeded 3 percent and usually was less than 2 percent. Since 2000, the rate has risen as high as a low 5 percent before dropping back to the 4 percent range as Taiwan struggles to adjust to outsourcing to mainland China. By human measures, Taiwan's growth was also a great success. For example, the literacy rate increased from 45 percent in 1946 to 93 percent in 1989; life expectancy went from 59 years in 1952 to 74 years in 1989 while the per capita caloric intake went from 2,078 calories to 3,070 calories in the same period. Living space per person went from 4.6 square meters to 23.8 square meters.[8] Further, Taiwan and the other "Asian Tigers" were able to achieve these successes despite having population densities among the highest in the world, a fact which contradicts the prevailing dogma that population density is an impediment to growth.

Employee Stock Ownership Plans (ESOP)

ESOPs are a leveraged buyout of a company on behalf of the employees. To simplify a complex process, a fund is set up to borrow the money with which to buy the company. As the loan is repaid from the profits of the firm, ownership is transferred to the employees, so that over time they become owners of their own firm. There are thousands of ESOPs in theory; however, there are a much smaller number in practice because the law allows ESOPs to function as a tax dodge, so many are set up with no intention of transferring real ownership. ENRON, for example, was an ESOP in name, but certainly not in fact; the owners had no intention of relinquishing their control.

Where there is a sincere intention to transfer real ownership to the workers, however, ESOPs tend to outperform their shareholder corporate cousins. The sign of this sincere intention is not so much the formality of the ESOP, but the culture of "open management" that is established within the firm. An outstanding example of this is the Springfield ReManufacturing Corp (SRC), which was originally a division of International Harvester, but was purchased by a group of its employees, headed by Jack Stack. These men had an idea of business that was completely different from the remote shareholder model of the modern corporation.

Of course, Stack and his colleagues would offer ownership to their employees, but this was just a means to an end:

> Part of the problem has been the tendency of companies to use stock merely as a form of compensation—a carrot to get people to work harder. In a company with a strong culture of ownership, stock is more than compensation. First and foremost, it's a vehicle for change. . . . Equity is used to involve people in the process of making a difference in the world. Why? Because business is not an end in itself. It's a means to an end.[9]

What Stack set out to create was a community of entrepreneurs, rather than just a collection of people with jobs; indeed, SRC wanted to do away with "jobs" and the "employee" mentality altogether. But the primary problem is that people have been trained to see themselves in terms of jobs rather than entrepreneurs; they see themselves as merely performing a function for somebody else, usually somebody very remote. To accomplish this goal, to create this community, SRC used two means: education and equity-sharing.

To educate the members of the firm (it would be wrong to say "employees"), Stack invented a system of informal but continuous education he called the Great Game of Business. If the workers are going to take responsibility for the firm, they must know the rules of business, and the Great Game was the means of teaching them these rules, from the simplest to the most complex. As Stack evaluates the results of this "game," he notes that "we've had dozens of employees rise from the shop floor . . . to top management positions, and they're far better qualified than a lot of MBAs I see."[10] The game required that the firm practice open-book management. If all members of the firm are to be responsible for the firm, then they all must have equal access to the books. Further, you cannot truly educate employees unless they can see how their actions affect the firm, and this is impossible without looking at the books. But the greatest benefit, as Jack Stack notes is that, "When you open your books—really open them—you also open your mind, and neither your mind nor your books will be closed again."[11]

Continuous education and open-book management frees the firm from the constraints of the division of labor, which confines each worker to just one task, and from the quasi-militaristic, "top-down" management, which confines responsibility to just one group. The results of this culture at SRC have been nothing short of phenomenal. In twenty years, they went from sales of $16 million to $185 million, with similar results for profit and shareholder equity. But it is in the area of shareholder equity that the firm really stands out, because all of the shares are owned by the workers. The company has 727 worker-owners, of whom only five were original members of the firm. The other 722 shareholders own 64 percent of the firm. This point is crucial, because "owning their work" must involve real ownership, and not just some psychic substitute. Equity-sharing defines the community, a community built on the premise that all the members of the community must share in the wealth that the community creates.

Other Examples

There are many other functioning examples of distributism in action: microbanking, mutual banks and insurance companies, buyers and producers cooperatives of every sort. This sample should be enough to show how distributism works in practice. Distributists are often accused of being "back to the land" romantics. The truth is otherwise. It is the capitalist who is the true romantic, because he believes in an ideal of which there is no functioning example; capitalism is never able to operate anywhere near its own principles; the mortality rates are simply too high. The distributist, on the other hand, is a hardheaded realist, believing in what he can see, putting his faith in systems that work in practice. In reality, this idealistic capitalism always ends up relying on government power and money to rescue it from its own idealistic excesses; the distributist relies on functioning systems to deal with reality. Distributism goes from success to success; capitalism goes from bailout to bailout.

19

Building the Ownership Society

Distributism and the Current Crisis

Discussions of what to do about the current crisis commonly take the form of an argument between "socialism" and "capitalism." However, such a discussion is flawed in both of its terms. Real socialism collapsed in 1989, and few would want to return to that horrific system. What is less well understood is that pure capitalism itself collapsed in 1929, never to rise again anywhere in the world. There are few citizens with any living memory of real capitalism, and the memories they have are generally unfavorable. Capitalism collapsed for the same reason as Communism, a victim of its own internal contradictions that caused chronic instability. Workers found the system unacceptable, to be sure, but so did the capitalists themselves, and few were sorry to see it go. Pure capitalism had proved itself toxic to both capital and labor, just as Belloc predicted it would in 1913.

The first task in reforming the system is to understand the system that we have—the system that is in full failure—and understand it apart from the ideological terms commonly used to describe it. The system that replaced capitalism was first a hyper-active Keynesianism, which was brought about by World War II and which lasted until the late 1970s. Keynesianism itself was then replaced by a pure mercantilism, the system that combines private privilege with public power and that so incited the wrath of Adam Smith. It is this mercantilism which finds itself in the midst of a full-blown collapse. Both the Keynesianism which replaced capitalism and the mercantilism which replaced Keynesianism depend on massive government controls and subsidies that are no longer practicable or sustainable. Nor can we go back to the capitalism of the 1920s without reliving the instability of that turbulent period.

If capitalism is not a viable alternative, if it represents a system that no living man has seen, why then do the arguments in its favor carry such weight? I believe the reasons are mostly ideological. Capitalists are quite willing to trot out libertarian arguments when dealing with some regulation or tax that they find odious, but they are just as willing to put such arguments aside when they seek some privilege or subsidy from the government. In this way, the most well-meaning of the libertarians serve as the fellow-travelers of the mercantilists. And although I have a great deal of respect for the libertarian arguments in general, in practice these arguments do not function apart from well-divided property, as the older, pre-Austrian libertarians realized.

We should devote a word or two to the passing of the corporate capitalist. I believe that it is already being shown that the great corporations are not economically efficient, as they claim, but only politically efficient; that is, they are able to concentrate political power in their own hands and therefore obtain great subsidies and privileges from the state; their greatest "efficiency" is their ability to pass their costs on to the environment and to the public purse; their "profits" are largely a creation of state power and subsidies.

One sign of this inefficiency, one of many such signs, comes in the matter of the provision of jobs. Since the capitalists are also internationalists, no less than were the Marxists, we are not surprised that the globalists have sent so many of our jobs abroad. This was supposed to lead to a corresponding increase of jobs in this country, but in fact, while it led directly to growth in finance, real estate, and insurance, these things cannot replace the jobs produced in the field, the forest, the fishery, the factory, and the mine; these are the primary sources of wealth for a nation, and every other profession must eat of the food they provide and use the things they make. It doesn't matter whether your system is capitalist, Communist, socialist, Keynesian, or Fascist; only these things can provide real wealth to a nation, and when we lose them, we lose nothing less than the ability to feed and clothe ourselves, and must depend on the kindness of foreign governments.

We need not dispute too much about whether the globalist system is passing; this is an empirical question and the answer will soon be given, as it was given for all the other systems. But there are several things we may learn from looking at what is common to all of these systems. The primary feature they share in common is that they were all new and clever ideas about how social systems work; that is to say, they were all very original *ideologies*. However, they embodied a false idea of originality. True originality comes not from novelty or inventing new "truths," but from applying old truths to new situations in creative and humane ways, ways that respects the soil in which the ideas are planted. This is always a local task, rather than a global one.

The Political Agenda of Distributism

Despite the obvious differences among these clever ideologies, there were actually four features that united them. The first was that each claimed to be scientific in the sense of physics or mathematics; that is, they were abstract ideas divorced from any actual reality of time and place, but purported to answer all questions in advance, regardless of the particularities of time and place. The second great claim of all these systems is that they were globalist and universalist. The capitalist, no less than the Communist, has his own *Internationale,* sung to the tune of a cash register, with accompaniment supplied by a chorus of the WTO, the EU, the World Bank, and the IMF. The third unifying feature is that they were all capitalistic, yes even, or especially, the Communists. That is, they all believed that human progress depended on great accumulations of capital placed in the hands of a comparatively few bureaucrats—whether public or private, it doesn't much matter—and that the people as a whole could not be trusted with their own money, or at least not with their own capital. The family farm, the small businessman—these became suspicious categories, or at best were marginalized. Finally, politics became a technical matter, a question of proper administration of rules that could be universally known by a select group of experts, preeminently economic experts but also social planners, city planners, and the like; that the only real role of politics was to select the proper experts and to provide them with public funds and public powers. The actual operation of government became more and more isolated from democratic processes, and some areas, such as monetary policy, became totally independent, or nearly. Moreover, since government was really just a collection of experts, it was best done from above, from the highest level possible.

Now, in thinking how creatively to apply the old truths to these new conditions, I think that we could do worse than simply to take these four features of the prevailing ideologies, and *do exactly the opposite.* So then, in place of a claim of physical science, we should *re-moralize* the markets. In place of globalist claims, we should *re-localize the economy.* In place of capitalist claims, we should *re-capitalize* the poor, the small farm, and the small businessman. And in place of the sterile politics of technique and expertise, we should *re-invigorate and re-localize* the political order. The first three of these items are the political agenda suggested by Philip Blond in his speech to the English Conservative Party, "The Civic State."[1] The fourth is specific to an America in which the federal government has all but displaced every other level of government, and turned them into mere administrative departments of an ever-growing state. Let us examine these four points in turn.

Of all these four points, *re-moralizing the markets* will appear most offensive to the economists. "We are scientists," they will say, "and we should no more be required to consult the moral order than is the physicist!" But this claim totally misunderstands the kind of science economic science is. It is indeed a science, but not a physical science. Rather, it is a humane science, one that deals with a particular set of human relationships, those necessary for the material provisioning of the family and the society. But in modern economics, the family, indeed the human person, disappears. Men and women—workers—become no more than a factor of production, like pigs or pig iron. The market for men, they tell us, is no different from the market for pigs. But in reducing men to pigs, you destroy not only the social order, but the economic order as well. After all, we do not ask the pigs to purchase the output of production; they are not our customers. But workers are, and without a just reward from their work, markets cannot be cleared. G. K. Chesterton put the problem like this:

Capitalism is contradictory as soon as it is complete, for the master is always trying to cut down what his servant demands, and hence is cutting down what his customer can spend. He is asking the same person to act in contradictory ways: he wishes to pay him as a pauper, but wants him to spend like a prince.[2]

The morality of markets is embodied in the concept of justice, not as something alien to the markets, but as something foundational. Without justice, the markets simply cannot achieve a stable balance between supply and demand. Unjust markets are chaotic markets, always staggering between boom and bust, spending too much today and too little tomorrow. Further, this lack of justice has another effect: no government can tolerate such chaotic markets. Hence, governments are forced to intervene in the markets, to increase their level of taxation, spending, and regulation. Government becomes the buyer of last resort, and the size, power, and cost of government constantly increases. This is why the growth of capitalism and the growth of government go hand in hand; they feed on each other. Or more accurately, they feed on the poor and the middle class. Taxes and regulations are a small part of a large business, but a large part of a small business. A corporation can simply establish a department to handle the paperwork, to deal with the bureaucrats. But an entrepreneur must give his own time, distracting him from his own business. Hence, all these regulations actually act as a protective fence around the corporations, protecting them from real competition from the entrepreneur. Capitalism claims to be a free-market system, but the historical reality is that the market has diminished and the government has grown under the care of the capitalists. *And there are no exceptions to this rule.*

Those who would shrink the government and grow the market must address the cause of government growth and market failure. And the cause is always and everywhere the same: the lack of morality in the markets. Justice is not something alien to economic science, but the principle of practical reason that keeps things reasonable. The economic theory that preached "greed is good" is shown to be neither good nor economic.

The gargantuan size of business and government brings me to

the second point, *re-localization of the markets*. As the great corporations grow, they become larger than the governments they deal with. National or even regional markets no longer satisfy them, no longer contain their appetite for power. These transnational corporations prefer transnational institutions, institutions that dwarf all but the largest and most powerful governments. Only certain governments, and certain large businesses, have any voice or influence in these organizations. Other national governments are asked—no, required—to surrender their powers to remote organizations. They are required to give up their own currencies, which is equivalent to giving up their sovereignty, at least over monetary and fiscal matters. Increasingly, they find themselves hemmed in by regulations drafted in places in which they have no power. Power in these organizations will be the servant of the larger clients, as is true in nearly every sort of organization.

There is a certain irony in this, for as the national states absorbed the functions of city and regional governments, so the national governments now find themselves surrendering their own sovereignty to international governments. Nationalism gives way to internationalism, and ordinary citizens, and their local governments, find themselves farther and farther away from the centers of power and influence. The whole process makes a mockery of democratic and national institutions.

But the process also makes a mockery of local markets, the markets that provide scope for the entrepreneurs and local leaders of a society. The transnational corporations colonize spaces that were once left to the small business and the farmer. The shop is replaced by the supermarket, the local factory by the remote sweatshop, even the family farm is replaced by the highly subsidized agribusiness. Local markets are the foundation, not only for strong economies, but also for strong societies. The local businessman contributes to his community a range of values that exceed the merely economic. These are values that the bureaucrat working for a transnational corporation never can contribute. As the space for local entrepreneurship shrinks, so do the opportunities for civic engagement and local institutions.

The building of local markets requires local capital. However, capitalism tends to concentrate wealth, not disburse it. In the United States, in 2007, the top 1 percent owned 35 percent of the wealth of the nation, and the top 5 percent owned 60 percent. But in terms of financial wealth, the kind of liquid wealth available for investment, the numbers are 42 percent and 70 percent. In other words, 95 percent of our citizens share just 30 percent of the liquid wealth. It should be pointed out that the last time the imbalance of wealth was this severe was in 1929.[3] I don't believe that these dates are an accident: severe recessions are triggered by severe imbalances; 1929 and 2007 share an imbalance in wealth distribution and a severe recession; the former, I believe, is the direct cause of the latter.

Aside from causing severe dislocations, the concentration of capital at the top, whether under capitalists or Communists, leaves very little room for local investment, for the dispersion of wealth and enterprise throughout the various communities that comprise the nation. By starving the local cities and regions of capital, their development is hampered, not only in the economic sense, but in the cultural and social sense as well. Therefore, re-capitalizing the poor, the farmer, the small businessman, the village, and the city, is an essential part—*the* essential part—of developing the nation.

Finally, we can note that all of these things, the concentration of capital, the internationalization of the economy, and the divorce of the economic from the moral and political orders leads to a concentration of power at the national and international levels. The cities and regions are reduced to mere administrative districts of the national state and the international institutions. But a strong polity is developed from the bottom up, not the top down. Traditions and institutions of civic responsibility and democracy grow first in the village and the city, and only later work their way up to the national and international levels. The liberal tradition of trying to impose order from the top is like trying to build a house by starting with the roof. To *re-invigorate* the political order we must follow the principle of subsidiarity; that is, we must transfer as much power and responsibility to the local levels of government as possible. Further, the purpose of the higher levels of government is to serve the lower levels, not be served by them. Strong local institutions, endowed with rights of their own and backed by citizens willing to defend those rights, are the best guarantee against national and international tyranny.

Distributism and Government

Critics of distributism often charge that the theory is no more than a variety of socialism. This charge is odd for two reasons: One, socialism is the theory that there should be no private property, while distributism is the theory that property ought to be spread as broadly as possible; the two are precisely opposite. Two, the actual practice of distributism, in Mondragón and other places, is more "libertarian" than anything the libertarians have been able to accomplish. Nevertheless, the critique cannot be passed off lightly because the very term *distributism* conjures up the specter of *redistribution*, the idea that some committee of bureaucrats will decide who will—and who will not—own property.

But in the main, distributism is not so much about what the government ought to do as about what it ought to stop doing. The claim of the distributist in this regard is not much different from the claim of the anarchist libertarian: it is government which fosters the accumulation of property into fewer and fewer hands. Indeed, without the aid and protection of government, the piles of capital could not have grown as high as they have. And the higher the piles of private capital grow, the thicker the walls of public power necessary to protect them. Big government and big capital go together, and this is a simple fact of our history, beyond all reasonable dispute.

That being said, there are clearly cases where government must, in fact, redistribute property. The case of Taiwan comes to mind, where the population was held in virtual slavery to a few landowners. The remarkable prosperity of that island is traceable to the decisive action of the "land to the tiller" program, which made most of the sharecroppers into independent farmers. Those who would defend the landowners and the sanctity of property over the misery and poverty of the people corrupt the very notion of property. Property is a sacred right, but not an absolute one. Every proper right is known by its limits, and an absolute right is not a right at all, but the seedbed of tyranny. Property that depends on the slavery of others is certainly not legitimate property. And in such egregious cases, the government can indeed take action.

And then there is the case of the entities deemed "too big to fail," or more accurately, too big to succeed without generous drafts from the public purse. It is quite legitimate to break up such companies and to distribute them either to the local or regional banks or to the employees. The same principle applies to the failed industrial giants that require public life support. They can be broken up and turned over to the workers through the simple expedient of placing contractual obligations for pay and pensions on the same level as the contractual obligations to the bondholders. Then we can see if the workers can run these factories any better than the geniuses in Detroit. If the similar experience in Argentina is any guide, they might do very well indeed. In that country, after the economic collapse of 2001, workers took over failed factories to establish *fabricas sin patrones*, (factories without bosses). They were able to convert the failed enterprises into successful businesses, thereby calling into question the usefulness of a management separated from actual labor.[4]

Finally, we can note that as long as capitalism endures, distributists may legitimately call on the power of government to limit its manifold excesses. For example, so long as there are monopolies, price-controls are a legitimate public response. Ideally, we would want to eliminate such monopolies that are not strictly necessary, but as long as the government protects monopolies, it is reasonable to ask for protection from monopolies.

All that being said, our main interest in dealing with government is to deal it out of the game. It is not that there would be no government—distributists are not anarchists—but compared to the size and scale of the current mercantilism, it would look a lot like "no government." Still there are functions which are properly left to the community and these would be left in place. Anyone who objects to any government whatsoever as a form of socialism ought not to pull that socialist lever in their home, the one that makes their waste disappear in a whirlpool into the socialized sewage treatment plant

You Say You Want a Devolution?

The principles of reform were outlined in the previous chapters. Here we summarize the major steps that need to be taken. It should be noted, however, that *devolution* is not *revolution,* although its impact is revolutionary. Distributist enterprises can exist side by side with other forms of business organization, just as they do today. But as the subsidies for the corporate state are eroded, so too is the power of both the state and the corporations.

Devolution as a Fiscal Problem

Conservatives express great frustration with the egregious violations of the Constitution by the legislatures and the courts, violations which ensure that power gravitates to the federal government, while the states become mere bureaucratic subdivisions of the federal apparatus rather than partners in a political union. In response, they call for a devolution, a return of power to the states. Many historical, political, and philosophical reasons could be advanced for the centralization of power, but at base this turns out to be a *fiscal* problem. Power follows property, as Daniel Webster noted. The political equivalent is that power follows funding, that it gravitates towards that level of government that has the most money to spend. When the federal government acquired the power to tax incomes with the Sixteenth Amendment in 1913—a source of funds with no natural limit—the rest of the Constitution gradually became irrelevant.

In order to implement subsidiarity in government, we must also have subsidiarity in the funding of government. That is, funding must start at the local level and be dispersed upward, rather than the other way round. Further, we must tax that which has no economic value, that is, the tax should fall primarily on economic rent and externalities (chapter 15). Economic rent can be confiscated with no negative economic consequences (except for the rentiers) and many positive ones. Externalities (the costs of a transaction charged to a third party not involved in the transaction, e.g., pollution) should be charged with the full cost of their mitigation. With any luck at all, the government will be sufficiently inefficient at mitigating externalities that businesses will prefer to perform the mitigation themselves and not pay the tax.

Economic rent is primarily embodied in ground rents (chapter 9).

Treated as a tax, ground rents are most efficiently collected at the local level, and indeed the bureaucracy to do so already exists. Obviously, there has to be national agreement on the methods used to value and assess ground rents and on the "split" between local, state, and the federal governments. But lower levels of government will then have an incentive to accept more responsibilities, rather than kick problems upstairs, because this justifies claiming a larger portion of the revenues, revenues which they themselves collect. Politically, the problem with a "ground-rent tax" is that it sounds like a "property tax," and that scares people. Once it is understood, however, that we are trading off the income tax for the ground tax, most people, I suspect, will see the advantage. They will have a tax easily predicted, easily collected, and local, without the government prying into the details of their lives.

Devolution and Deficits

Moreover, it is not just the problem of getting government to live within reduced means, there is also the problem of the enormous debt that must be paid off (or significantly reduced) if both sanity and subsidiarity are to be restored. The federal debt is, as I write this, $12.4 trillion and rising rapidly. The interest on that debt exceeds half a trillion dollars; after the defense budget, it is the largest expenditure of the federal government and will soon be the largest. These are monies that must be paid out before a single bullet is bought or a single bridge rebuilt. Thus, we seem to face intractable problems. On the one hand, we would like to reduce both taxes and the expenditures of government, and on the other we must pay a seemingly insurmountable debt from these reduced revenues. Nor is that all. Our infrastructure is aging and much of it needs to be rebuilt, at enormous expense. The freeway system, for example, was begun in the 1950s, and many parts are nearing the end of their useful life. The same goes for many other parts of the infrastructure, such as levees and dams. This will put enormous pressures on any attempts to rein in the budget.

To add to the problems, we are about to face the retirement of the postwar baby-boom generation, which will arrive like a fiscal tsunami on the Social Security and Medicare budgets. In the face of all these problems, it would seem that we need not lower taxes, but higher; not a devolution to the states, but an even more powerful central government empowered to tackle these enormous and growing problems. However, this would be to gorge on the medicine that made us sick in the first place, which can only make us sicker. How then should we confront these problems?

No real progress can be made if this debt is not eliminated, or at least substantially reduced. In thinking about the debt, one has to think about money itself. In chapter 7 we noted that the creation of money is the private monopoly of the banks. This money is created out of thin air, and represents no prior savings or production. Yet, it forms a claim against things that have been produced. In the case of government debt, the banks lend money they invent, but demand payment in the equivalent of real goods and services. Hence, the government must tax real goods and services and turn over the money to the creditors. But this will become increasingly less of a possibility in the near future.

Monetary Reform

One of the greatest forces for the unjust accumulation of property is this fractional reserve banking system, which grants a monopoly privilege to a small group of people, namely the bankers and their allies. These private citizens have the power to create out of thin air nearly all the money in circulation. Such a system is intolerable on both moral and economic grounds, and must result in periodic credit crises, as greed and necessity move bankers to create more money than the economy needs or can be reasonably "repaid" (chapter 7). That last word is in quotes because you can't "repay" what was never paid in the first place, or repay in real goods a "debt" that was only an accounting entry on the books of some bank.

I do not believe that an ownership society can be reconciled with such a money system. The creation of money is a public power, and the public ought to take it back. Coining money into being ought to be the sole authority of the community, which includes those communities known as governments, or indeed any goods-producing community that can back its money with a store of goods.

There is no reason why the federal government should not create its own money and spend it into circulation for capital projects. Capital projects, in the main, create more wealth than they cost, hence there would be little inflationary effect. The federal government could also act as a banker to the states and cities to lend them money, at little or no interest, to finance their own capital needs. This would shift the power inherent in capital projects back to the states and cities. In any case, control of the money supply should not be in private hands; it is a public power, and the public should take it back.

Localizing the Economy

Industrial Reform. Political subsidiarity would mean little if the industrial system remained concentrated; it does no good to collect taxes locally if the production of goods, and therefore the production of taxable values, is not also widespread. In chapter 16, we noted the problems and inefficiencies of the current system, a system that is highly dependent on subsidies and externalized costs. Once these subsidies are removed, it is unlikely that the current production model could actually produce anything at a profit. Localized production will follow in the wake of the demise of the subsidies.

Indeed, the large corporations themselves have already opted for distributed production, divesting themselves of actual factories and seeking to retain centralized control through cheap transportation and legal control of the patents. The highly integrated, vertical model pioneered by Henry Ford has been in decline for some time; distributism is the order of the day in corporate America. Unfortunately, they have dispersed the factories around the world, rather than around the country. Nevertheless, this still plants the seeds of their own demise. One day, the workers in Vietnam making shoes for Nike will realize that they can ignore the patents, rip the "swooshtika" off the shoes, and sell them locally for a tenth of the price, while paying their workers three times the wages and still making twice the profit. Indeed, the Chinese have already discovered this, and all the talk of "piracy" will not change these facts.

Agrarian Reform. Distributists are frequently accused of being romantic agrarians. We are agrarians, but we are not romantics. *Agrarian* means, in this context, not moving everybody back to the farm, but restoring the proper relationship between town and country. Contrary to corporate opinion, a tomato does not taste better if it is picked green and shipped a thousand miles before it is consumed. But apart from the question of flavor, there is the economic inefficiency inherent in such a system, inefficiencies that are covered up by subsidies.

One thing is for certain: neither the environment nor the economy will tolerate much longer the current system of factory farming. The cabbage grown in Oregon and consumed in Texas consumes more energy in its growing, picking, transportation, and marketing than it supplies in calories. If the energy inputs—the chemical fertilizer, the heavy equipment, the fuel for machinery and transportation, and so forth—were properly priced and the subsidies removed, this transcontinental cabbage would not be a paying proposition. And it will not be in the very near future. Even today, the system depends on an easily exploitable workforce that does not participate in the benefits offered to the rest of society, creating a vast underclass whose legal status is ambiguous, even as their numbers proliferate.

Trade Reform. Trade is a basic part of the human condition; no family, firm, city, or nation can or should be self-sufficient. But trade is only good when it really is *trade,* that is, when you earn enough to buy the things you purchase. A "trade" that is based on borrowing to finance consumption is not really trade at all, but the prelude to bankruptcy. This is a basic fact overlooked by our trade policies, which are based on a doctrinaire application of the basic "free-trade" theory, called the theory of comparative advantage. The people who argue the theory most strenuously, however, seem to be the ones least familiar with it. The theory is valid only under three conditions: one, that capital is relatively immobile; two, that there is full employment in both countries; and three, that trade is balanced between both countries (chapter 17). Absent these conditions, a doctrinaire "free trade" makes both parties poorer, as the poor in both countries are played off against each other. In the United States, it has resulted in a hollowing out of our industrial base. But no country can expect to grow prosperous except by making things; if we lose this ability, we guarantee ourselves and our children a life of dependence and poverty.

Without the necessary conditions, an insistence on free trade ceases to be a useful economic paradigm and becomes a mere political ideology. When conditions are less than the ideal of the pure theory, then trade between nations must be managed, just as trade between firms is managed. We should make those deals which make sense, and reject the others.

Distributism and Reform

Since the current system is not sustainable, *it will be reformed,* one way or the other. The only question is whether we shall get out in front of the collapse and begin an informed movement towards sanity. Since the Enlightenment, the world has experimented with laissez-faire capitalism, socialism, Communism, Keynesianism, and mercantilism. While each of these systems contains some partial truth, they are all insufficient to the whole truth. All of these systems have been weighed in the balance of history and found wanting. It is time to return to a more natural system, and that is system is, I believe, distributism, or something very like it.

For the past few decades, distributists have mostly withdrawn from the purely economic debates to rest their case on moral and social claims. This is, of course, a necessary aspect of the problem. These claims cannot be made credible, however, unless there is also a credible economic argument behind them. As Cardinal Joseph Ratzinger (before becoming Pope Benedict XVI) stated,

> A morality that believes itself able to dispense with the technical knowledge of economic laws is not morality but moralism. As such it is the antithesis of morality. A scientific approach that believes itself capable of managing without an ethos misunderstands the reality of man. Therefore it is not scientific.[5]

My intention in writing this book is to demonstrate that distributism is a robust economic theory, demonstrated by actual practice, and capable of tackling the difficult and sophisticated problems that we face. I hope that this book will enable the distributist to enter the debate and stand his ground against all comers: socialist, capitalist, Austrian, Keynesian, or whomever.

This is the distributist moment. We must seize this moment; it will not come again. We must arm ourselves with both the moral and technical knowledge that will be required to reform our world and preserve our freedom. For, make no mistake, although all these other answers have been tried and found wanting, there is yet another answer: slavery. Slave societies have proven themselves stable over long periods of time, and so provide a solution, no matter how distasteful to our Christian heritage, to the problems of social and economic stability. In the end, the question will be, as Belloc predicted it would, between freedom and slavery.

Notes

Chapter 1

1. Alfred Marshall, *Marshall: Principles of Economics* (Library of Economics and Liberty, 1890), book 1, chap. 1, sec. 1, http://www.econlib.org/library/Marshall/marP.html.

Chapter 2

1. National Bureau of Economic Research, "Business Cycle Expansions and Contractions," http://www.nber.org/cycles.html (accessed May 17, 2006).
2. Eric Tymoigne, "Business Cycles," (Fresno, CA: Economic Policy Institute, 2007).
3. Hilaire Belloc, *The Servile State* (Indianapolis: Liberty Classics, 1913), 107–121.
4. Friedrich A. von Hayek, *The Road To Serfdom* (Chicago: University of Chicago Press, 1944).
5. Ibid., 54.
6. Rafe Champion, "The Road to Serfdom: Fifty Years On," The Rathouse, http://www.the-rathouse.com/hayserf.html (accessed June 7, 2008).
7. J. M. Keynes, *The General Theory of Employment, Interest, and Money* (New York: Harcourt, 1935), 372.

Chapter 3

1. J. E. Alvey, "A Short History of Economics As a Moral Science," *Journal of Markets and Morality* 2, no. 1 (1999), http://www.acton.org/publicat/m_and_m/1999_spr/alvey.html.

2. Milton Friedman, *Essays in Positive Economics* (Chicago: University of Chicago Press, 1953), 4.

3. D. S. Long, *Divine Economy: Theology and the Market* (New York: Routledge, 2000), 2.

4. David Hume, *An Enquiry Concerning Human Understanding*, vol. 37, *The Harvard Classics*, http://www.bartleby.com/37/3/19.html.

5. A. A. Chafuen, *Faith and Liberty: The Economic Thought of the Late Scholastics* (New York: Lexington Books, 2003), 24.

6. Ibid., 25 (italics in original).

7. Long, *Divine Economy: Theology and the Market*, 4–5.

8. Ibid., 5.

9. C. M. A. Clark, "Economic Insights from the Catholic Social Thought Tradition: Towards a More Just Economy," 2005.

Chapter 4

1. C. M. A. Clark, "Catholic Social Thought and the Economic Problem," http://www.pust.edu/oikonomia/pages/febb2000/Clark.htm (accessed March 12, 2006).

2. R. L. Heilbroner, *The Making of Economic Society* (New Jersey: Prentice Hall, 2002), 6.

3. Clark, "Catholic Social Thought and the Economic Problem."

4. J. D. Mueller, *Redeeming Economics: Rediscovering the Missing Element* (Wilmington, DE: ISI Books, 2010), 83.

Chapter 5

1. There are noneconomic ways to add wealth to a nation, such as plundering other countries.

2. There is actually a third source of income, *economic rent*, or an amount paid beyond what it takes to keep an asset in productive use. Economic rent introduces some serious complications, and will be dealt with in a later chapter.

3. There may be noneconomic or exogenous causes for a particular recession, such as flood, famine, or plague.

Chapter 6

1. E. K. Hunt, *History of Economic Thought: A Critical Perspective* (Armonk, NY: M. E. Sharpe, 2002), 5.

2. R. W. Faulhaber, "The Rise and Fall of 'Self-Interest,'" *Review of Social Economy* 63, no. 3 (September 2005), 418.

3. Aristotle, *Nicomachean Ethics* (New York: Modern Library, 1947), sec. 1139a 10.

4. Ibid., sec. 1129b, 25.

5. Ibid., sec. 1252b, 11.

6. Ibid., sec. 1253a, 26.

7. Ibid., sec. 1130b, 31–33.

8. Ibid., sec. 1131a, 25–29.

9. Corrective justice is also known as commutative justice, due to a mistranslation in the Middle Ages. "Commutative" has become the more common term, but we will use "corrective" as closer to Aristotle's original intention.

10. Ibid., sec. 1132b, 19–21.

11. Ibid., sec. 1131a, 25–31.

12. Cf. K. Polanyi, *The Great Transformation: The Political and Economic Origins of Our Time* (Boston: Beacon Press, 1944).

Chapter 7

1. Ibid., 75.

2. Hugh Stretton, *Economics: A New Introduction* (London: Pluto Press, 1999), 692.

3. Dorothy Nichols and Ann Marie Gonczy, *Modern Money Mechanics: A Workbook on Bank Reserves and Deposit Expansion* (n.p., The Federal Reserve Bank of Chicago, 1992), 3.

4. Ibid., 7–12.

5. William Greider, *Secrets of the Temple: How the Federal Reserve Runs the Country* (New York: Simon & Schuster, 1987), 276.

6. Ibid., 245.

7. "The Federal Reserve System: Purposes and Functions" (The Federal Reserve System, June 2005), 4.

8. Stephen Zarlenga, *The Lost Science of Money: The Mythology of Money, The Story of Power* (Valatie, NY: American Monetary Institute, 2002), 581.

9. Alex Von Muralt, "The Wörgl Experiment with Depreciating Money," *Reinventing Money*, (1934), http://www.reinventingmoney.com/worglExperiment.php.

Chapter 8

1. Paul Heyne, Peter J. Boettke, and David L. Prychitko, *The Economic Way of Thinking*, 10th ed. (Delhi, India: Pearson Education, 2003), 462.

2. Stretton, *Economics: A New Introduction*, 404.

3. G. K. Chesterton, *The Collected Works of G.K. Chesterton* (San Francisco: Ignatius Press, 1987), 59.

4. Hunt, *History of Economic Thought: A Critical Perspective*, 132.

5. Mueller, *Redeeming Economics*, 311–12.

Chapter 9

1. Heyne, Boettke, and Prychitko, *The Economic Way of Thinking*.

2. G. Small, *An Aristotelian Construction of the Social Economy of Land* (Sydney, Australia: University of Technology, 2000), 52, http://adt.lib.uts.edu.au/public/adt-NTSM20030811.163754/.

3. The time-preference simply means that most people would prefer to have a dollar today rather than a dollar at some future date, say a year from now. In order to induce them to part with their dollar today, there must be an expectation of receiving more than a dollar at a future date. For example, if the lowest amount that will induce them to part with their dollar is $1.10 over the course of a year, then their time-preference is equal to 10 percent, and any investment they purchase will have to be at a price discounted by 10 percent.

4. H. George, *Progress and Poverty* (New York: Robert Schalkenbach Foundation, 1880), 263.

Chapter 10

1. Adam Smith, *An Inquiry into the Nature and Causes of the Wealth of Nations* (Amherst, NY: Prometheus Books, 1991), 55.

2. Thomas Aquinas, *Summa Theologica* (Allen, TX: Christian Classics, 1911), sec. II-II, query 57, art. 3.

3. Ibid., sec. II-II, query 66, art. 3.

4. Ibid.

5. Ibid., sec. II-II, query 66, art. 3, addendum 3.

6. Ibid., sec. II-II, query 66, art. 7.

7. Smith, *An Inquiry into the Nature and Causes of the Wealth of Nations,* 45.

8. G. K. Chesterton, *What's Wrong with the World* (San Francisco: Ignatius Press, 1994), 42.

Chapter 11

1. Pope Leo XIII, *Rerum Novarum* (Boston: St. Paul Books and Media), par. 6.

2. Ibid., par. 63.

3. Ibid., par. 65.

4. Ibid., par. 66.

5. J. B. Clark, *The Distribution of Wealth: A Theory of Wages, Interest, and Profits* (New York: Augustus M. Kelly, 1899), 2.

6. Ibid., 3 (italics in original).

7. Ibid., 94.

8. Ibid., 101.

9. Ibid., 195.

10. Ibid., 16.

11. Smith, *An Inquiry into the Nature and Causes of the Wealth of Nations,* 70.

12. Stretton, *Economics: A New Introduction,* 407–8.

13. Pope John Paul II, *Laborem Exercens,* 1981, par. 13 (italics in original).

14. Cf. J. C. Bogle, *The Battle for the Soul of Capitalism* (New Haven, CT: Yale University Press, 2005), xix.

Chapter 15

1. Fred Foldvary, "Intellectual Tyranny of the Status Quo," Econ Journal Watch, http://www.econjournalwatch.org/pdf/FoldvaryIntellectualTyrannyApril2005.pdf.

Chapter 16

1. Pankaj Ghemawat, "How Business Strategy Tamed the 'Invisible Hand,'" Harvard Business School Working Knowledge, July 22, 2002, http://hbswk.hbs.edu/item/3019.html.
2. Kevin Carson, "Industrial Policy: New Wine in Old Bottles," Center for a Stateless Society, http://c4ss.org/content/78.
3. Throughout this discussion, I am indebted to Kevin Carson's *Organization Theory: A Libertarian Perspective* (Booksurge, 2008).
4. I should note here, in passing, that goods sold internally do not have a sales tax, giving the corporation a government-sponsored advantage over other forms of organization.
5. Bogle, *The Battle for the Soul of Capitalism*, xix.
6. Ibid., 31–2.
7. Carson, *Organization Theory: A Libertarian Perspective*, 198.
8. Carson, "Industrial Policy: New Wine in Old Bottles."
9. Naomi Klein, *No Logo* (New York: Picador, 2002), 3.

Chapter 17

1. Center for Medicare and Medicaid Services, "NHE Fact Sheet National Health Expenditure Data," National Health Expediture Data, http://www.cms.hhs.gov/NationalHealthExpendData/25_NHE_Fact_Sheet.asp.
2. "OECD Health Data 2008: Frequently Requested Data," http://www.oecd.org/document/16/0,3343,en_2649_34631_2085200_1_1_1_37407,00.html.

Chapter 18

1. "All In This together," *The Economist*, March 26, 2009, http://www.economist.com/business/displaystory.cfm?story_id=13381546.

2. R. Matthews, *Jobs of Our Own: Building a Stakeholder Society* (Sydney, Australia: Comerford and Miller, 1999), 194.

3. Ibid., 185.

4. Ibid., 195.

5. Mondragón Cooperative Corporation, "2007 Annual Report," December 31, 2007, http://www.mcc.es/ing/magnitudes/memoria2007.pdf.

6. P. Ginsborg, *Italy and Its Discontents: Family, Civil Society, State, 1980–2001* (New York: Palgrave Macmillion, 2003), 17.

7. J. Jacobs, *Cities and the Wealth of Nations: Principles of Economic Life* (New York: Random House, 1985), 100.

8. S. W. Y. Kuo, "Economic Development of the Republic of China on Taiwan," in *Agriculture on the Road to Industrialization* (Baltimore: John Hopkins University Press, 1995), 334.

9. J. Stack, *A Stake in the Outcome: Building a Culture of Ownership for the Long-Term Success of Your Business* (New York: Doubleday, 2003), 5.

10. Ibid., 9.

11. Ibid.

Chapter 19

1. Phillip Blond, The Civic State," ResPublica, http://www.respublica.org.uk/articles/civic-state.

2. Chesterton, *The Collected Works of G.K. Chesterton*, Vol. 5, 59.

3. Edward N. Wolff, "Recent Trends in Household Wealth in the United States: Rising Debt and the Middle-Class Squeeze—An Update to 2007," Levy Economics Institute of Bard College, March, 2010

4. Monique Gabrielle Maes y Salazar , "Occupar, Resisti, Producir: Occupy, Resist, Produce: The Story of the Fabricas Sin Patron—Argentina's Factories without Bosses," April 23, 2009, Kansas City Indymedia, http://kcindymedia.org/articles/6

5. Joseph Ratzinger, "Market Economy and Ethics," Acton Institute, http://www.acton.org/publications/occasionalpapers/publicat_occasionalpapers_ratzinger.php.

Select Bibliography

"All In This together." *The Economist,* March 26, 2009. http://www.economist.com/business/displaystory.cfm?story_id=13381546.

Alvey, James E. "A Short History of Economics As a Moral Science." *Journal of Markets and Morality* 2, no. 1 (1999). http://www.acton.org/publicat/m_and_m/1999_spr/alvey.html.

Aquinas, Thomas. *Summa Theologica* (Allen, TX: Christian Classics, 1911).

Aristotle. *Nicomachean Ethics* (New York: Modern Library, 1947).

Belloc, Hilaire. *The Servile State* (Indianapolis: Liberty Classics, 1913).

Blond, Phillip. "The Civic State" ResPublica. http://www.respublica.org.uk/articles/civic-state.

Bogle, John C. *The Battle for the Soul of Capitalism* (New Haven, CT: Yale University Press, 2005).

Carson, Kevin. "Industrial Policy: New Wine in Old Bottles," Center for a Stateless Society. http://c4ss.org/content/78.

———. *Organization Theory: A Libertarian Perspective* (Charleston, SC: Booksurge, 2008).

Center for Medicare and Medicaid Services. "NHE Fact Sheet National Health Expenditure Data." *National Health Expediture Data.* http://www.cms.hhs.gov/NationalHealthExpendData/25_NHE_Fact_Sheet.asp.

Chafuen, Alejandro A. *Faith and Liberty: The Economic Thought of the Late Scholastics* (New York: Lexington Books, 2003).

Champion, Rafe. "The Road to Serfdom: Fifty Years On," The Rathouse. http://www.the-rathouse.com/hayserf.html, June 7, 2008.

Chesterton, G. K. *The Collected Works of G. K. Chesterton* (San Francisco: Ignatius Press, 1987).

———. *What's Wrong with the World* (San Francisco: Ignatius Press, 1994).

Clark, Charles M. A. "Catholic Social Thought and the Economic Problem," March 12, 2006. http://www.pust.edu/oikonomia/pages/febb2000/Clark.htm.

———. "Economic Insights from the Catholic Social Thought Tradition: Towards a More Just Economy," 2005.

Clark, J. B. *The Distribution of Wealth: A Theory of Wages, Interest, and Profits* (New York: Augustus M. Kelly, 1899).

Faulhaber, Robert W. "The Rise and Fall of 'Self-Interest.'" *Review of Social Economy* 63, no. 3 (September 2005): 405–422.

Foldvary, Fred. "Intellectual Tyranny of the Status Quo," Econ Journal Watch. http://www.econjournalwatch.org/pdf/FoldvaryIntellectual-TyrannyApril2005.pdf.

Friedman, Milton. *Essays in Positive Economics* (Chicago: University of Chicago Press, 1953).

George, Henry. *Progress and Poverty* (New York: Robert Schalkenbach Foundation, 1880).

Ghemawat, Pankaj. "How Business Strategy Tamed the 'Invisible Hand.'" Harvard Business School Working Knowledge, July 22, 2002. http://hbswk.hbs.edu/item/3019.html.

Greider, William. *Secrets of the Temple: How the Federal Reserve Runs the Country* (New York: Simon & Schuster, 1987).

Hayek, Frederick A. von. *The Road To Serfdom* (Chicago: University of Chicago Press, 1944).

Heilbroner, Robert L. *The Making of Economic Society* (New Jersey: Prentice Hall, 2002).

Heyne, Paul, Peter J. Boettke, and David L. Prychitko. *The Economic Way of Thinking.* 10th ed. (Delhi, India: Pearson Education, 2003).

Hume, David. *An Enquiry Concerning Human Understanding.* Vol. 37. *The Harvard Classics.* http://www.bartleby.com/37/3/19.html.

Hunt, E. K. *History of Economic Thought: A Critical Perspective* (Armonk, NY: M. E. Sharpe, 2002).

Jacobs, Jane. *Cities and the Wealth of Nations: Principles of Economic Life* (New York: Random House, 1985).

John Paul II. *Laborem Exercens,* 1981.

Keynes, John M. *The General Theory of Employment, Interest, and Money* (New York: Harcourt, 1935).

Klein, Naomi. *No Logo* (New York: Picador, 2002).

Kuo, S. W. Y. "Economic Development of the Republic of China on Taiwan." In *Agriculture on the Road to Industrialization* (Baltimore: John Hopkins University Press, 1995).

Leo XIII. *Rerum Novarum* (Boston: St. Paul Books and Media, 1891).

Long, D. Stephen. *Divine Economy: Theology and the Market* (New York: Routledge, 2000).

Maes y Salazar, Monique Gabrielle. "Occupar, Resistir, Producir: Occupy, Resist, Produce: The Story of the Fabricas sin Patron—Argentina's Factories without Bosses," April 23, 2009 at Kansas City Indymedia. http://kcindymedia.org/articles/6.

Marshall, Alfred. *Marshall: Principles of Economics.* Library of Economics and Liberty, 1890. http://www.econlib.org/library/Marshall/marP.html.

Matthews, Race. *Jobs of Our Own: Building a Stakeholder Society* (Sydney, Australia: Comerford and Miller, 1999).

Mondragón Cooperative Corporation. "2007 Annual Report," December 31, 2007, at http://www.mcc.es/ing/magnitudes/memoria2007.pdf.

Mueller, John. D. *Redeeming Economics* (Wilmington, DE: ISI Books, 2010).

National Bureau of Economic Research. "Business Cycle Expansions and Contractions," May 17, 2006, at http://www.nber.org/cycles.html.

Nichols, Dorothy, and Ann Marie Gonczy. *Modern Money Mechanics: A Workbook on Bank Reserves and Deposit Expansion* (Chicago: The Federal Reserve Bank of Chicago, 1992).

"OECD Health Data 2008—Frequently Requested Data" http://www.oecd.org/document/16/0,3343,en_2649_34631_2085200_1_1_1_37407,00.html.

Polanyi, Karl. *The Great Transformation: The Political and Economic Origins of Our Time* (Boston: Beacon Press, 1944).

Ratzinger, Joseph. "Market economy and ethics." http://www.acton.org/publications/occasionalpapers/publicat_occasionalpapers_ratzinger.php.

Small, Garick. *An Aristotelian Construction of the Social Economy of Land* (Sydney, Australia: University of Technology, Sydney, 2000). http://adt.lib.uts.edu.au/public/adt-NTSM20030811.163754/.

Smith, Adam. *An Inquiry into the Nature and Causes of the Wealth of Nations* (Amherst, NY: Prometheus Books, 1991).

Stack, Jack. *A Stake in the Outcome: Building a Culture of Ownership for the Long-Term Success of Your Business* (New York: Doubleday, 2003).

Stretton, Hugh. *Economics: A New Introduction* (Stirling, VA: Pluto Press, 1999).

"The Federal Reserve System: Purposes and Functions." The Federal Reserve System, June 2005.

Zarlenga, Stephen. *The Lost Science of Money: The Mythology of Money, The Story of Power* (Valatie, NY: American Monetary Institute, 2002).

Index

Index